Archana and Other Sanskrit Prayers

with English translation

I0241452

Archana and Other Sanskrit Prayers

with English Translation

Published by
Mata Amritanandamayi Center
P.O. Box 613, San Ramon, CA 94583-0613 USA

In India:
www.amritapuri.org
inform@amritapuri.org

In Europe:
www.amma-europe.org

In US:
www.amma.org

Tyāgenaike amṛtatvamānaśuḥ

By renunciation alone immortality is attained

(Kaivalya Upaniṣad)

Contents

Benefits of the Archana 5
Mānasa Puja 6
Mātā Amṛtānandamayi Aṣṭottara Śata Nāmāvali 12
Śrī Lalitā Sahasranāmāvali 32
Śrī Mahiṣāsuramardini Stotram 182
Śrī Lalitā Sahasranāma Stotram 194
Śrī Lalitā Triśatī Stotra 228
Ārati 272
Bhagavad Gītā – Chapter 8 276
Bhagavad Gītā – Chapter 15 286
Yagna Mantra 295
Guru Stotram 296
Devī Bhujaṅgam 302
Annapūrṇa Stotram 310
Closing Prayers 317
Pronunciation Guide 320

Benefits of the Archana

The daily chanting of Lalitā Sahasranāmā is intended to bring prosperity to the family and peace to the world. It is supposed to be a powerful tool to minimize the karmic effects of our past actions. The chanting will also enhance our one-pointedness, thereby helping us deepen our devotion and spiritual practices. Lowering of physical, mental, and emotional stress, bestowing good health, and increasing the life span, etc. are other benefits of chanting the 1000 names of Sri Lalitā Paramesvari. The chanting not only purifies the practitioner, but also cleanses the atmosphere. It is said that Devi will protect those who chant the Lalitā Sahasranāmā with devotion every day and that they will never face a shortage of food and basic necessities.

–Amma

6
Mānasa Puja

Amma's instructions for mental worship of one's Beloved Deity during meditation.

Sit in a comfortable asana (posture) and try to feel a deep peace filling your being. Breathe slowly, deeply, consciously for 2–3 minutes. Chant Aum three times with eyes closed. While chanting, imagine taking Aum from the navel upwards to the Sahasrara; also imagine the bad mental dispositions and bad thoughts within us flowing out. Then while praying "Amma, Amma..." with devotion, love, and tearful longing, imagine that the Divine Mother is standing before you, smiling and looking at you compassionately. For a minute enjoy Mother's exquisite beauty, visualizing every part of Her divine form. Prostrate at Mother's Lotus Feet, feeling the touch of your forehead on Her Holy Feet. Pray to Her, "O Mother, I take refuge in You. You are the only lasting Truth and support for me. You alone can give me real peace and joy. Never forsake me, never leave me!"

Then visualize the resplendent form of Devi on the inside of your palms. Rays of compassion from Devi's eyes envelop you. Rub your face and from the face downwards with the palms. Feel that a divine energy is permeating you, and feel all misfortunes, all inauspiciousness being driven away.

Throughout this puja, continuously repeat with your lips, but without making any sound, "Amma, Amma, Amma, leave me not, forsake me not."

Imagine now that you are bathing Mother. As you pour water on Mother's head, watch the water flow down over each part of Her form until it reaches Her Lotus Feet. Then do ablutions with milk, ghee, honey, sandal paste, rose water, etc. With each item enjoy the beauty of Her form. Imagine that through offering these materials, you are offering your own purified mind to Mother.

Next, do ablutions with vibhuti (sacred ash). Watch how it slowly reaches

Mother's Feet. Then shower flowers on Mother's head. Take a nice towel and wipe Her face and body. Adorn Her with a beautiful sari, as if you are dressing up your own child. Pray to Her, "O Mother, come sit in my heart. Only if You sit in my heart, can I tread the right path."

Apply perfume on Devi. Adorn Her with Ornaments: earrings, necklace, belt, anklets, etc. Apply kumkum (saffron) on Her forehead. Place a crown bedecked with jewels on Her head. Garland Mother. Enjoy watching Mother's peerless beauty, and let your glance pass from Her head down to Her feet and from Her feet to Her head again. Like a child, talk to Mother about all kinds of things. Pray to Her, "O Mother, You are pure love. I am too impure to deserve Your Grace. I know that my egoism and selfishness must be repelling to You. Still, bear with me. Mother, please be with me. You are the holiest river. I am a stagnant, filthy pond. You flow to me and purify me, overlooking my shortcomings and forgiving my mistakes."

With sandal paste, write Om on Mother's feet. Offer flowers three times. Now, after reciting the Dhyānam (p.10) in a meditative mood, begin to chant the Sahasranāmāvali, beginning with the Om śrī matre namaḥ. (If chanting in a group, respond to each chant with Om parāśaktyai namah.) As you chant each name, imagine that you are picking a flower from your heart, and mentally offer the flower at Mother's Lotus Feet. (The flower represents your own pure heart.) When the Thousand Names have been chanted, sit erect silently for a few minutes, imagining that divine vibrations are spreading throughout your being.

Now, offer sweet porridge as naivedya (sacred food offering) for the Mother with your own hands and imagine that She relishes it. The real naivedya is your pure love for the Mother. If you can sing, sing then a song offering to the Mother. Imagine that hearing the song, the Mother is dancing. Dance along with Her. Suddenly in the midst of the dance, She leaves you and runs away. Run after Her until you catch hold of Her. Cry out to Her: "O

Mother, why are You forsaking me? Why do You allow me to perish in this forest of samsara? I am being burnt in the fire of worldliness. Come, lift me up and save me." Mother now stops running and She calls you, holding out Her arms towards you. Run to Her and embrace Her. Sit on Mother's lap. Take complete freedom with Mother, as a child would with its own mother, caressing Her body and Lotus Feet, plaiting Her hair, etc. Ask Mother to never tease you like this again. Tell Her all your grievances and your anxieties. Tell Mother that you will never again allow Her to leave you. Pray to Her: "O Mother, I am offering myself at Your Lotus Feet. Make me an ideal instrument of Yours. I do not want anything of this world. My only desire is to behold Your Divine form and to be in Your company. Give me eyes that see nothing but Your beauty. Give me a mind that revels in nothing but You. Let Your will be my will, let Your thoughts be my thoughts, Your words my words. Whatever I do, even eating and sleeping, let all my actions have only one aim—that of merging in You. Let me become as selfless and loving as You." Constantly talking and praying like this, fix your mind on the Divine Mother's form.

Wave lighted camphor before Mother, who stands before you smiling, Her eyes full of compassion. Imagine that you are offering all your good and your bad qualities, and the whole of yourself to Her.

Do pradakshina (circumambulation) and prostrate at Mother's Lotus Feet with the prayer in your heart: "O Mother of the Universe, You are my only refuge. I surrender to You."

Chant the peace invocations: asatomā sadgamaya, lokāh samastāh sukhino bhavantu and purnamadah purnamidam. After seeing Her there, while feeling peace and fullness of heart, bow to Her and to the place where you sat. Conclude the puja. If possible, meditate on Her form for some more time.

Om peace, peace, peace!

Mātā Amṛtānandamayi Aṣṭottara Śata Nāmāvali

The Hundred and Eight Names of Mata Amritanandamayi

Dhyāyāmo dhavalāvaguṇṭhanavatīṁ tejomayīm naiṣṭhikīṁ
snigdhāpāṅga vilokinīm bhagavatīṁ mandasmita śrī mukhīṁ
vātsalyāmṛta varṣiṇīm sumadhuraṁ saṅkīrtanālāpinīṁ
śyāmāṅgīṁ madhu sikta sūktīṁamṛtānandātmikām īśvarīṁ

We meditate (on Mata Amritanandamayi), who is clad with a white garment, who is effulgent, who is ever-established (in Truth), whose glances beam with binding love, who is the seat of the six godly qualities, whose radiant smile adorns Her face with auspiciousness, who incessantly showers the nectar of affection, who sings devotional songs most sweetly, whose complexion resembles that of rain clouds, whose words are soaked in honey, who is bliss immortal, and who is the Supreme Goddess Herself.

I bow down to Amma,

1 Om pūrṇa brahma svarūpiṇyai namaḥ

...who is the complete manifestation of the absolute Truth.

2 Om saccidānanda mūrtaye namaḥ

...who is existence, knowledge, and bliss embodied.

3 Om ātmā rāmāgragaṇyāyai namaḥ

...who is supreme among those who revel in the inner Self.

4 Om yoga līnāntarātmane namaḥ

...whose Self is merged in yoga (the union of the Self with Brahman).

5 Om antar mukha svabhāvāyai namaḥ

...who is inwardly drawn by Her very nature.

6 Om turya tuṅga sthalījjuṣe namaḥ

...who dwells in the top most plane of consciousness known as 'turya'.

7 Om prabhā maṇḍala vīta yai namaḥ

...who is totally surrounded by divine light.

8 Om durāsada mahaujase namaḥ

...whose greatness is unsurpassable.

9 Om tyakta dig vastu kālādi sarvāvacceda rāśaye namaḥ

...who has risen above all the limitations of space, matter, and time.

10 Om sajātīya vijātīja svīya bheda nirākṛte namaḥ

...who is devoid of all kinds of differences.

11 Om vāṇī buddhi vimṛgyāyai namaḥ

...whom speech and intellect cannot apprehend.

12 Om śaśvad avyakta vartmane namaḥ

...whose path is eternally undefined.

13 Om nāma rūpādi śūnyāyai namaḥ

...who is devoid of name and form.

14 Om śūnya kalpa vibhūtaye namaḥ

...to whom the yogic powers are of no importance (like the whole world is unimportant when in dissolution).

15 Om ṣaḍaiśvarya samudrāyai namaḥ

...who has the auspicious marks of the six godly qualities (affluence, valour, fame, auspiciousness, knowledge, and dispassion).

16 Om dūrī kṛta ṣaḍ ūrmaye namaḥ

...who is devoid of the six modifications of life (birth, existence, growth, change or evolution, degeneration, and destruction).

17 Om nitya prabuddha saṁśuddha nirmuktātma prabhāmuce namaḥ

...who is emanating the light of the Self, eternal, conscious, pure, and free.

18 Om kāruṇyākula cittāyai namaḥ

...whose heart is full of mercy.

19 Om tyakta yoga suṣuptaye namaḥ

...who has given up the yogic sleep.

20 Om kerala kṣmāvatīrṇāyai namaḥ

...who has incarnated in the land of Kerala.

21 Om mānuṣa strī vapurbhṛte namaḥ

...who has a feminine human body.

22 Om dharmiṣṭha suguṇānanda damayantī svayam bhuve namaḥ

...who has incarnated of Her own will as the daughter of the virtuous Sugunananda and Damayanti.

23 Om mātā pitṛ cirācīrṇa puṇya pūra phalātmane namaḥ

...who was bom to Her parents as a result of their many virtuous deeds over many lives.

24 Om niśśabda jananī garbha nirgamādbhuta karmaṇe namaḥ

...who miraculously kept silence when She came out of Her mother's womb.

25 Om kālī śrī kṛṣṇa saṅkāśa komala śyāmala tviṣe namaḥ

...who has the beautiful dark complexion reminiscent of Kali and Krishna.

26 Om cira naṣṭa punar labdha bhārgava kṣetra sampade namaḥ

...who is the wealth (treasure) of Kerala (land of Bhargava) lost for a long time and now regained.

27 Om mṛta prāya bhṛgu kṣetra punar uddhita tejase namaḥ
...who is the life of Kerala, which was almost dying and is now resurrected.

28 Om sauśīlyādi guṇākṛṣṭajaṅgama sthāvarālaye namaḥ
...who by Her noble qualities, like good behaviour, attracts the whole creation.

29 Om manuṣya mṛga pakṣyādi sarva saṁsevitāṅghraye namaḥ
...whose feet are served by humans, animals, birds, and all others.

30 Om naisargika dayā tīrtha snāna klinnāntarātmane namaḥ
...whose inner Self is always bathing in the holy river of mercy.

31 Om daridra janatā hasta samarpita nijāndhase namaḥ
...who offered Her own food to the poor.

32 Om anya vaktra pra bhuktānna pūrita svīya kukṣaye namaḥ
...whose stomach becomes full when others have their meals.

33 Om samprāpta sarva bhūtātma svātma sattānubhūtaye namaḥ
...who attained the experience that Her Self is one with the Self of all beings.

34 Om aśikṣita svayam svānta sphurat kṛṣṇa vibhūtaye namaḥ
...who knew all about Krishna without being taught.

35 Om acchinna madhurodāra kṛṣṇa līlānusandhaye namaḥ
...who continuously contemplated on the sweet sports of Lord Krishna.

36 Om nandātmaja mukhāloka nityotkaṇṭhita cetase namaḥ
...whose mind ever craves to see the face of the Son of Nanda (Krishna).

37 Om govinda viprayogādhi dāva dagdhāntarātmane namaḥ
...whose mind was burning in the fire of the agony of separation from Govinda.

38 Om viyoga śoka sammūrcchā muhur patita varṣmaṇe namaḥ
...who often fell down unconscious, due to the grief of non union with Krishna.

39 Om sārameyādi vihita śuśrūṣā labdha buddhaye namaḥ
...who regained consciousness by the nursing given by dogs and other animals.

40 Om prema bhakti balākṛṣṭa prādur bhāvita śārṅgiṇe namaḥ
...whose supreme love drew Krishna by force, as it were, to manifest Himself before Her.

41 Om kṛṣṇa loka mahāhlāda dhvasta śokāntarātmane namaḥ
...who was relieved of Her agony by the immense joy of the vision of Krishna.

42 Om kāñcī candraka manjīra vaṁśī śobhi svabhū dṛśe namaḥ
...who had the vision of the shining form of Krishna, with golden ornaments such as girdles, anklets, peacock feather, and flute.

43 Om sārvatrika hṛṣīkeśa sānnidhya laharī spṛśe namaḥ
...who felt the all pervading presence of Hrisikesa (Krishna).

44 Om susmera tan mukhāloka vismerotphulla dṛṣṭaye namaḥ
...whose eyes remained wide open with joy on beholding Krishna's smiling face.

45 Om tat kānti yamunā sparśa hṛṣṭa romāṅga yaṣṭaye namaḥ
...whose hair stood on end when She touched the river of His beauty.

46 Om apratīkṣita samprāptādevī rūpopalabdhaye namaḥ
...who had an unexpected vision of the Divine Mother.

47 Om pāṇī padma svapadvīṇā śobhamānāmbikā dṛśe namaḥ
...who had the vision of the Divine Mother holding the veena in Her lotus hand.

48 Om devī sadyas tirodhāna tāpa vyathita cetase namaḥ

...who became very sorrowful on the Divine Mother's sudden disappearance.

49 Om dīna rodana nir ghoṣa dīrṇa dikkarṇa vartmane namaḥ

...whose sorrowful wailing was rending the ears of the four quarters.

50 Om tyaktānna pāna nidrādi sarva daihika dharmaṇe namaḥ

...who gave up all bodily activities like eating, drinking, sleeping.

51 Om kurarādi samānīta bhakṣya poṣita varṣmaṇe namaḥ

...whose body was nourished by the food brought by birds and animals.

52 Om vīṇā niṣyanti saṅgīta lālita śruti nālaye namaḥ

...whose ears became filled by the waves of divine melodies emanating from the veena (in the hands of the Divine Mother).

53 Om apāra paramānanda laharī magna cetase namaḥ

...whose mind was merged in the intoxicating, limitless, supreme bliss.

54 Om caṇḍikā bhīkarākāra darśanālabdha śarmaṇe namaḥ

...whose mind was filled with peace by the vision of the terrible form of the Divine Mother (Chandika).

55 Om śānta rūpāmṛtajharī pāraṇā nirvṛtātmane namaḥ

...who was filled with ecstasy drinking from the ambrosial river of the blissful aspect (of the Divine Mother).

56 Om śāradā smārakāśeṣa svabhāva guṇa sampade namaḥ

...whose nature and qualities remind us of Sri Sarada Devi.

57 Om prati bimbita cāndreya śāradobhaya mūrtaye namaḥ

...in whom is reflected the dual form of Sri Ramakrishna and Sri Sarada Devi.

58 Om tannāṭakābhinayana nitya raṅgayitātmane namaḥ

...in whom we can see the play of these two re enacted.

59 Om cāndreya śāradā kelī kallolita sudhābdhaye namaḥ

...who is the ocean of ambrosia in which the waves of the various plays of Sri Ramakrishna and Sri Sarada Devi arise.

60 Om uttejita bhṛgu kṣetra daiva caitanya raṁhase namaḥ

...who has enhanced the divine potentialities of Kerala.

61 Om bhūyaḥ pratyavaruddhārṣa divya saṁskāra rāśaye namaḥ

...who has re established the eternal, divine values enunciated by the rishis.

62 Om aprākṛtāt bhūtānanta kalyāṇa guṇa sindhave namaḥ

...who is an ocean of divine qualities which are natural, wondrous, infinite.

63 Om aiśvarya vīrya kīrti śrī jñāna vairāgya veśmaṇe namaḥ

...who is the embodiment of rulership, valour, fame, auspiciousness, knowledge, dispassion; the six characteristics of divine personification.

64 Om upātta bāla gopāla veṣa bhūṣā vibhūtaye namaḥ

...who assumed the form and qualities of Bala Gopala (the child Krishna).

65 Om smera snigdha kaṭākṣāyai namaḥ

...whose glances are most sweet and loving.

66 Om svairādyuṣita vedaye namaḥ

...who leads programmes playfully on the dais.

67 Om piñcha kuṇḍala mañjīra vaṁśikā kiṅkiṇī bhṛte namaḥ

...who wore all the ornaments, the peacock feather, the earrings, the anklets, and the flute, like Krishna.

68 Om bhakta lokākhilā bhīṣṭa pūraṇa prīṇanecchave namaḥ

...who is keen to please the world of devotees by fulfilling all their desires.

69 Om pīṭhārūḍha mahādevī bhāva bhāsvara mūrtaye namaḥ

...who in the mood of the Great divine Mother, seated on the pitham (Divine seat), looks divinely resplendent.

70 Om bhūṣanāmbara veṣa śrī dīpya mānāṅga yaṣṭaye namaḥ

...whose entire body shines, adorned by ornaments and unique dress like that of the Divine Mother.

71 Om suprasanna mukhāmbhoja varābhayada pāṇaye namaḥ

...who has a bright, beaming face, as beautiful as a lotus flower, and who holds Her hand in the posture of blessing.

72 Om kirīṭa raśanākarṇa pūra svarṇa paṭī bhṛte namaḥ

...who wears all the various gold ornaments and the crown, like the Divine Mother.

73 Om jihva līḍha mahā rogi bībhatsa vraṇita tvace namaḥ

...who licks with Her tongue the festering ulcers of people stricken with terrible diseases.

74 Om tvag roga dhvaṁsa niṣṇāta gaurāṅgāpara mūrtaye namaḥ

...who, like Sri Chaitanya, is an adept in removing skin diseases.

75 Om steya hiṁsā surāpānā dyaśeṣādharma vidviṣe namaḥ

...who strongly disapproves of bad qualities like stealing, injuring others, using intoxicants, etc.

76 Om tyāga vairagya maitryādi sarva sadvāsanā puṣe namaḥ

...who encourages the cultivation of good qualities, like renunciation, dispassion, love, etc.

77 Om pādāśrita manorūḍha dussaṁskāra rahomuṣe namaḥ

...who steals away all bad tendencies from the hearts of those who have taken refuge in Her Lotus Feet.

78 Om prema bhakti sudhāsikta sādhu citta guhājjuṣe namaḥ

...who resides in the cave of the hearts of the pious that are drenched with the nectar of devotion.

79 Om sudhāmaṇi mahā nāmne namaḥ

...who has the great name Sudhamani.

80 Om subhāṣita sudhā muce namaḥ

...whose speech is as sweet as ambrosia.

81 Om amṛtānanda mayyākhyā janakarṇa puṭa spṛśe namaḥ

...whose name, as Amritanandamayi, resounds all over the world.

82 Om dṛpta datta viraktāyai namaḥ

...who is indifferent to the offerings by vain and worldly people.

83 Om namrārpita bhubhukṣave namaḥ

...who accepts the food offered by devotees with humility.

84 Om utsṛṣṭa bhogi saṅgāyai namaḥ

...who is disinclined to be in the company of pleasure seekers.

85 Om yogi saṅga riraṁsave namaḥ
...who cherishes the company of yogis.

86 Om abhinandita dānādi śubha karmā bhivṛddhaye namaḥ
...who encourages good actions, like charity, etc.

87 Om abhivandita niśśeṣa sthira jaṅgama sṛṣṭaye namaḥ
...who is worshipped by the sentient and insentient beings of the world

88 Om protsāhita brahmavidyā sampradāya pravṛttaye namaḥ
...who encourages the learning of Brahmavidya, the science of the Absolute through the traditional Guru disciple lineage.

89 Om punar āsādita śreṣṭha tapovipina vṛttaye namaḥ
...who brought back the great way of living of the sages of the forests.

90 Om bhūyo gurukulā vāsa śikṣaṇotsuka medhase namaḥ
...who is keen on re establishing the 'gurukula' way of education.

91 Om aneka naiṣṭhika brahmacāri nirmātṛ vedhase namaḥ
...who is a mother to many, many life long brahmacharins.

92 Om śiṣya saṅkrāmita svīya projvalat brahma varcase namaḥ

...who has transmitted Her divine brilliance to Her disciples.

93 Om antevāsi janāśeṣa ceṣṭā pātita dṛṣṭaye namaḥ

...who watches over all the actions of the disciples.

94 Om mohāndha kāra sañcāri lokā nugrāhi rociṣe namaḥ

...who delights in blessing the worlds, moving like a heavenly light, dispelling the darkness.

95 Om tamaḥ kliṣṭa mano vṛṣṭa svaprakāśa śubhāśiṣe namaḥ

...who sheds the light of Her blessings on the hearts of those suffering in the darkness of ignorance.

96 Om bhakta śuddhānṭa raṅgastha bhadra dīpa śikhā tviṣe namaḥ

...who is the bright flame of the lamp kindled in the pure heart of devotees.

97 Om saprīthi bhukta bhaktaughanyarpita sneha sarpiṣe namaḥ

...who enjoys drinking the ghee offered by the devotees.

98 Om śiṣya varya sabhā madhya dhyāna yoga vidhitsave namaḥ
...who likes to sit with the disciples in meditation.

99 Om śaśvalloka hitācāra magna dehendriyāsave namaḥ
...whose body and senses are always acting for the good of the world.

100 Om nija puṅya pradānānya pāpādāna cikīrṣave namaḥ
...who is happy in exchanging Her own merits with the demerits of others.

101 Om para svaryāpana svīya naraka prāpti lipsave namaḥ
...who is happy in exchanging heaven with hell for the relief of others.

102 Om rathotsava calat kanyā kumārī martya mūrtaye namaḥ
...who is Kanya Kumari in human form, as on the occasion of the chariot festival.

103 Om vimo hārṇava nirmagna bhṛgu kṣetrojjihīrṣave namaḥ
...who is anxious to uplift the land of Kerala, which is immersed in the ocean of ignorance.

104 Om punassantā nita dvaipāyana satkula tantave namaḥ
...who has extended the great lineage of sage Veda Vyasa.

105 Om veda śāstra purāṇetihāsa śāśvata bandhave namaḥ

...who is the eternal friend of the vedic knowledge and all other spiritual texts.

106 Om bṛghu kṣetra samun mīlat para daivata tejase namaḥ

...who is the divine glory of the awakening land of Kerala.

107 Om devyai namaḥ

...who is the Great Divine Mother.

108 Om premāmṛtānandamayyai nityam namo namaḥ

...who is full of divine love and immortal bliss, adoration again and again

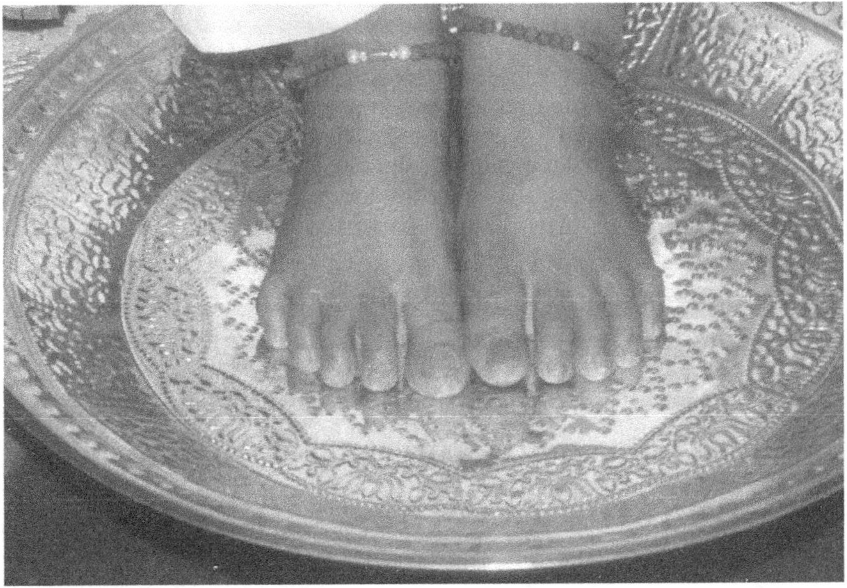

Śrī Lalitā Sahasranāmāvali

The Thousand Names of the Divine Mother in Mantra Form

Dhyānam – Meditation Verses

Sindūrāruṇa vigrahām tri nayanām māṇikya mauli sphurat
tārānāyaka śekharām smita mukhīm āpīna vakṣoruhām
pāṇibhyām alipūrṇa ratna caṣakam raktotpalam bibhratīm
saumyām ratna ghaṭastha rakta caraṇām dhyāyet parām ambikām

O Mother Ambika, I meditate on Your resplendent red form with three sacred eyes, wearing a sparkling crown jewel and the crescent moon and displaying a sweet smile, with Your large breasts brimming with motherly love holding in each hand jewel studded vessels decked with red lotus flowers which are encircled by bees. and with Your red lotus feet resting on a golden jar filled with jewels!

Dhyāyet padmāsanasthām vikasita vadanām padma patrāyatākṣīm
hemābhām pītavastrām kara kalita lasad hema padmām varāṅgīm
sarvālaṅkāra yuktām satatam abhayadām bhaktanamrām bhavānīm
śrī vidyām śānta mūrtim sakala sura nutāmsarva sampat pradātrīm

O Mother, let me meditate on Your beautiful form with the color of gold, with a beaming face and large lotus eyes, sitting in the lotus flower wearing a yellow garment and resplendent with all the ornaments, holding a golden lotus in Your hand, worshipped by the bowing devotees and always giving refuge! Let me meditate on You, O Sri Vidya, embodiment of peace, the object of worship by all the devas, and the bestower of all the riches!

Sakuṅkuma vilepanām alika cumbi kastūrikām
samanda hasitekṣaṇām saśara cāpa pāśāṅkuśām
aśeṣa jana mohinīm aruṇa mālya bhūṣojvalām
japā kusuma bhāsurām japavidhau smaredambikām

O Mother of the Universe, as 1 sit for japa, let me remember Your form with the beauty of the hibiscus flower, wearing a red garland and sparkling ornaments, smeared with red saffron, shining with a mark of musk on Your forehead whose fragrance is attracting the bees, holding in Your hands the bow and the arrow, the noose and the goad, and displaying a gentle smile, throwing sweet glances around, and beguiling everyone!

Aruṇām karuṇā taraṅgitākṣīm
dhṛta pāśāṅkuśa puṣpa bāṇa cāpām
aṇimādibhir āvṛtām mayūkhai
raham ityeva vibhāvaye maheśīm

O Great Goddess, let me imagine that I am one with Your glorious red form, surrounded by the golden rays from Anima and the other eight divine glories, holding the noose and the goad, the bow and the arrows of flowers, with eyes in which rise waves of compassion!

Nāmāvali

I bow down to Śrī Lalitā, ...

1. Om śrī mātre namaḥ
...who is the auspicious Mother.

2. Om śrī mahā rājñyai namaḥ
...who is the Empress of the Universe.

3. Om śrīmat siṁhāsaneśvaryai namaḥ
...who is the Queen of the most glorious throne.

4. Om cid agni kuṇḍa sambhūtāyai namaḥ
...who was born in the fire pit of Pure Consciousness.

5. Om deva kārya samudyatāyai namaḥ
...who is intent on fulfilling the wishes of the gods.

6. Om udyad bhānu sahasrābhāyai namaḥ
...who has the radiance of a thousand rising suns.

7. Om catur bāhu samanvitāyai namaḥ

...who is four armed.

8. Om rāga svarūpa pāśāḍhyāyai namaḥ

...who is holding the rope of love in Her hand.

9. Om krodhā kārāṅkuś ojjvalāyai namaḥ

...who shines, bearing the goad of anger.

10. Om mano rūpekṣu kodaṇḍāyai namaḥ

...who holds in Her hand a sugarcane bow that represents the mind.

11. Om pañca tanmātra sāyakāyai namaḥ

...who holds the five subtle elements as arrows.

12. Om nijāruṇa prabhā pūra majjad brahmāṇḍa maṇḍalāyai namaḥ

...who immerses the entire universe in the red effulgence of Her form.

13. Om campakāśoka punnāga saugandhika lasat kacāyai namaḥ

...whose hair has been adorned with flowers like campaka, etc.

14. Om kuruvinda maṇi śreṇī kanat koṭīra maṇḍitāyai namaḥ

...who is resplendent with a crown adorned with rows of kuruvinda gems.

15. Om aṣṭamī candra vibhrāja dalika sthala śobhitāyai namaḥ

...whose forehead shines like the crescent moon of the eighth night of the lunar half month.

16. Om mukha candra kalaṅkābha mṛganābhi viśeṣakāyai namaḥ

...who wears a musk mark on Her forehead which shines like the spot in the moon.

17. Om vadana smara māṅgalya gṛha toraṇa cillikāyai namaḥ

...whose eyebrows shine like the archways leading to the house of Kama, the god of love, which Her face resembles.

18. Om vaktra lakṣmī parīvāha calan mīnābha locanāyai namaḥ

...whose eyes possess the luster of the fish that move about in the stream of beauty flowing from Her face.

19. Om nava campaka puṣpābha nāsā daṇḍa virājitāyai namaḥ

...who is resplendent with a nose that has the beauty of a newly blossoming campaka flower.

20. Om tārā kānti tiraskāri nāsābharaṇa bhāsurāyai namaḥ

...who shines with a nose ornament that excels the luster of the venus.

21. Om kadamba mañjarī kḷpta karṇapūra manoharāyai namaḥ

...who is captivating, wearing bunches of kadamba flowers as ear ornaments.

22. Om tāṭaṅka yugalī bhūta tapanoḍupa maṇḍalāyai namaḥ

...who wears the sun and the moon as a pair of large earrings.

23. Om padma rāga śilādarśa paribhāvi kapola bhuve namaḥ

...whose cheeks excel mirrors made of rubies in their beauty.

24. Om nava vidruma bimba śrī nyakkāri radana cchadāyai namaḥ

...whose lips excel freshly cut coral and bimba fruit in their reflective splendor.

25. Om śuddha vidyāṅkurākāra dvija paṅkti dvayojjvalāyai namaḥ

...who has radiant teeth which resemble the buds of pure knowledge.

26. Om karpūra vīṭikāmoda samākarṣi digantarāyai namaḥ

...who is enjoying a camphor laden betel roll, the fragrance of which is attracting people from all directions.

27. Om nija sallāpa mādhurya vinirbhartsita kacchapyai namaḥ

...who excels even the veena of Sarasvati in the sweetness of Her speech.

28. Om manda smita prabhā pūra majjat kāmeśa mānasāyai namaḥ

...who submerges even the mind of Kamesha (Lord Shiva) in the radiance of Her smile.

29. Om anākalita sādṛśya cibuka śrī virājitāyai namaḥ

...whose chin cannot be compared to anything (because of its unparalleled beauty).

30. Om kāmeśa baddha māṅgalya sūtra śobhita kandharāyai namaḥ

...whose neck is adorned with the marriage thread tied by Kamesha.

31. Om kanakāṅgada keyūra kamanīya bhujānvitāyai namaḥ

...whose arms are beautifully adorned with golden armlets.

32. Om ratna graiveya cintāka lola muktā phalānvitāyai namaḥ

...whose neck is resplendent with a gem studded necklace with a pearl locket.

33. Om kāmeśvara prema ratna maṇi pratipaṇa stanyai namaḥ

...who gives Her breasts to Kameshvara in return for the gem of love He bestows on Her.

34. Om nābhyālavāla romāli latā phala kuca dvayyai namaḥ

...whose breasts are the fruits on the creeper of the fine hairline that starts in the depths of Her navel and spreads upwards.

35. Om lakṣya roma latā dhāratā sumunneya madhyamāyai namaḥ

...who has a waist, the existence of which can only be inferred by the fact that the creeper of Her hairline springs from it.

36. Om stana bhāra dalan madhya paṭṭa bandha vali trayāyai namaḥ

...whose abdomen has three folds which form a belt to support Her waist from breaking under the weight of Her breasts.

37. Om aruṇāruṇa kausumbha vastra bhāsvat kaṭī taṭyai namaḥ

...whose hips are adorned with a garment as red as the rising sun, which is dyed with an extract from safflower blossoms.

38. Om ratna kiṅkiṇikā ramya raśanā dāma bhūṣitāyai namaḥ

...who is adorned with a girdle which is decorated with many gem studded bells.

39. Om kāmeśa jñāta saubhāgya mārdavoru dvayānvitāyai namaḥ

...the beauty and softness of whose thighs are known only to Kamesha, Her husband.

40. Om māṇikya mukuṭākāra jānu dvaya virājitāyai namaḥ

...whose knees are like crowns shaped from the precious red manikya jewel (a kind of ruby).

41. Om indra gopa parikṣipta smara tūṇābha jaṅghikāyai namaḥ

...whose calves gleam like the jewel covered quiver of the God of Love.

42. Om gūḍha gulphāyai namaḥ

...whose ankles are hidden.

43. Om kūrma pṛṣṭha jayiṣṇu prapadānvitāyai namaḥ

...whose feet have arches that rival the back of a tortoise in smoothness and beauty.

44. Om nakha dīdhiti sañchanna namajjana tamoguṇayai namaḥ

...whose toenails give out such a radiance that all the darkness of ignorance is dispelled from those devotees who prostrate at Her feet.

45. Om pada dvaya prabhā jāla parākṛta saroruhāyai namaḥ

...whose feet defeat lotus flowers in radiance.

46. Om śiñjāna maṇi mañjīra maṇḍita śrī padāmbujāyai namaḥ

...whose auspicious lotus feet are adorned with gem studded golden anklets that tinkle sweetly.

47. Om marālī manda gamanāyai namaḥ

...whose gait is as slow and gentle as that of a swan.

48. Om mahā lāvaṇya śevadhaye namaḥ

...who is the treasure house of beauty.

49. Om sarvāruṇāyai namaḥ

...who is entirely red in complexion.

50. Om anavadyāṅgyai namaḥ
...whose body is worthy of worship.

51. Om sarvābharaṇa bhūṣitāyai namaḥ
...who is resplendent with all types of ornaments.

52. Om śiva kāmeśvarāṅkasthāyai namaḥ
...who sits in the lap of Shiva, who is the conqueror of desire.

53. Om śivāyai namaḥ
...who bestows all that is auspicious.

54. Om svādhīna vallabhāyai namaḥ
...who keeps Her husband always under Her control.

55. Om sumeru madhya śṛṅgasthāyai namaḥ
...who sits on the middle peak of Mount Sumeru.

56. Om śrīman nagara nāyikāyai namaḥ
...who is the Mistress of the most auspicious (or prosperous) city.

57. Om cintāmaṇi gṛhāntasthāyai namaḥ

...who resides in a house built of the wish fulfilling gem.

58. Om pañca brahmāsana sthitāyai namaḥ

...who sits on a seat made of five Brahmas.

59. Om mahā padmāṭavī saṁsthāyai namaḥ

...who resides in the great lotus forest.

60. Om kadamba vana vāsinyai namaḥ

...who resides in the kadamba forest.

61. Om sudhā sāgara madhyasthāyai namaḥ

...who resides in the center of the ocean of nectar.

62. Om kāmākṣyai namaḥ

...whose eyes awaken desire, who has beautiful eyes.

63. Om kāma dāyinyai namaḥ

...who grants all wishes.

64. Om devarṣi gaṇa saṅghāta stūyamānātma vaibhavāyai namaḥ
...whose might is the subject of praise by multitudes of gods and sages.

65. Om bhaṇḍāsura vadhodyukta śakti senā samanvitāyai namaḥ
...who is endowed with an army of shaktis intent on slaying Bhandasura.

66. Om sampatkarī samārūḍha sindhura vraja sevitāyai namaḥ
...who is attended by a herd of elephants ably commanded by Sampatkari.

67. Om aśvārūḍhādhiṣṭhitāśva koṭi koṭibhir āvṛtāyai namaḥ
...who is surrounded by a cavalry of several million horses which are under the command of the shakti Ashvarudha.

68. Om cakra rāja rathārūḍha sarvāyudha pariṣkṛtāyai namaḥ
...who shines in Her chariot Chakraraja, equipped with all kinds of weapons.

69. Om geya cakra rathārūḍha mantriṇī pari sevitāyai namaḥ
...who is served by the shakti Mantrini riding the Geyachakra chariot.

70. Om kiri cakra rathārūḍha daṇḍanāthā puras kṛtāyai namaḥ
...who is escorted by the shakti Dandanatha, seated in the Kirichakra chariot.

71. Om jvālā mālinikākṣipta vahni prākāra madhyagāyai namaḥ

...who has taken position at the center of the fortress of fire created by the goddess Jvalamalini.

72. Om bhaṇḍa sainya vadhodyukta śakti vikrama harṣitāyai namaḥ

...who rejoices at the valor of the shaktis who are intent on destroying the forces of Bhandasura.

73. Om nityā parākramāṭopa nirīkṣaṇa samutsukāyai namaḥ

...who delights in seeing the might and the pride of Her nitya deities.

74. Om bhaṇḍa putra vadhodyukta bālā vikrama nanditāyai namaḥ

...who delights in seeing the valor of the goddess Bala who is intent on killing the sons of Bhanda.

75. Om mantriṇyambā viracita viṣaṅga vadha toṣitāyai namaḥ

...who rejoices at the destruction, in battle, of the demon Vishanga by the shakti Mantrini.

76. Om viśukra prāṇa haraṇa vārāhī vīrya nanditāyai namaḥ

...who is pleased with the prowess of Varahi who took the life of Vishukra.

77. Om kāmeśvara mukhāloka kalpita śrī gaṇeśvarāyai namaḥ

...who gives rise to Ganesha by a glance at the face of Kameshvara.

78. Om mahā gaṇeśa nirbhinna vighna yantra praharṣitāyai namaḥ

...who rejoices when Ganesha shatters all obstacles.

79. Om bhaṇḍāsurendra nirmukta śastra pratyastra varṣiṇyai namaḥ

...who showers counter weapons to each weapon fired at Her by Bhandasura.

80. Om karāṅguli nakhotpanna nārāyaṇa daśākṛtyai namaḥ

...who created from Her fingernails all ten incarnations of Narayana (Vishnu).

81. Om mahā pāśupatāstrāgni nirdagdhāsura sainikāyai namaḥ

...who burned the armies of the demons in the fire of the Mahapashupata missile.

82. Om kāmeśvarāstra nirdagdha sabhaṇḍāsura śūnyakāyai namaḥ

...who burned and destroyed Bhandasura and his capital Shunyaka with the mighty Kameshvara missile.

83. Om brahmopendra mahendrādi deva saṁstuta vaibhavāyai namaḥ

...whose many powers are extolled by Brahma, Vishnu, Shiva and other gods.

84. Om hara netrāgni sandagdha kāma sañjīvanauṣadhyai namaḥ

...who became the life giving medicine for Kamadeva (the god of love) who had been burned to ashes by the fire from Shiva's eye.

85. Om śrīmad vāgbhava kūṭaika svarūpa mukha paṅkajāyai namaḥ

...whose lotus face is the auspicious vagbhavakuta (a group of syllables of the panchadasakshari mantra).

86. Om kaṇṭhādhaḥ kaṭi paryanta madhya kūṭa svarūpiṇyai namaḥ

...who from Her neck to Her waist is of the form of the madhyakuta (the middle six syllables of the panchadasakshari mantra).

87. Om śakti kūṭaikatāpanna kaṭyadhobhāga dhāriṇyai namaḥ

...whose form below the waist is the shaktikuta (the last four syllables of the panchadasakshari mantra).

88. Om mūla mantrātmikāyai namaḥ

...who is the embodiment of the mulamantra (the panchadasakshari mantra).

89. Om mūla kūṭa traya kalebarāyai namaḥ

...whose (subtle) body is made of the three parts of the panchadasakshari mantra.

90. Om kulāmṛtaika rasikāyai namaḥ

...who is especially fond of the nectar known as kula.

91. Om kula saṅketa pālinyai namaḥ

...who protects the code of rituals of the path of yoga known as Kula.

92. Om kulāṅganāyai namaḥ

...who is well born (who is from a good family).

93. Om kulāntasthāyai namaḥ

...who resides in Kulavidya.

94. Om kaulinyai namaḥ

...who belongs to the Kula.

95. Om kula yoginyai namaḥ
...who is the deity in the Kulas.

96. Om akulāyai namaḥ
...who does not have a family.

97. Om samayāntasthāyai namaḥ
...who resides inside Samaya (mental worship).

98. Om samayācāra tatparāyai namaḥ
...who is attached to the Samaya form of worship.

99. Om mūlādhāraika nilayāyai namaḥ
...whose principal abode is the Muladhara chakra.

100. Om brahma granthi vibhedinyai namaḥ
...who breaks through the knot of Brahma.

101. Om maṇipūrāntar uditāyai namaḥ
...who emerges in the Manipura chakra.

102. Om viṣṇu granthi vibhedinyai namaḥ
...who breaks through the knot of Vishnu.

103. Om ājñā cakrāntarālasthāyai namaḥ
...who resides at the center of the Ajna chakra.

104. Om rudra granthi vibhedinyai namaḥ
...who breaks through the knot of Shiva.

105. Om sahasrārāmbujārūḍhāyai namaḥ
...who ascends to the thousand petaled lotus.

106. Om sudhā sārābhi varṣiṇyai namaḥ
...who pours out streams of ambrosia.

107. Om taḍil latā sama rucyai namaḥ
...who is as beautiful as a flash of lightning.

108. Om ṣaṭ cakropari saṁsthitāyai namaḥ
...who resides above the six chakras.

109. Om mahā saktyai namaḥ

...who is greatly attached to the festive union of Shiva and Shakti.

110. Om kuṇḍalinyai namaḥ

...who has the form of a coil.

111. Om bisa tantu tanīyasyai namaḥ

...who is fine and delicate as the fiber of the lotus.

112. Om bhavānyai namaḥ

...who is the wife of Shiva.

113. Om bhāvanāgamyāyai namaḥ

...who is unattainable through imagination or thought.

114. Om bhavāraṇya kuṭhārikāyai namaḥ

...who is like an axe to clear the jungle of samsara.

115. Om bhadra priyāyai namaḥ

...who is fond of all auspicious things, who gives all auspicious things.

116. Om bhadra mūrtaye namaḥ

...who is the embodiment of auspiciousness or benevolence.

117. Om bhakta saubhāgya dāyinyai namaḥ

...who confers prosperity on Her devotees.

118. Om bhakti priyāyai namaḥ

...who is fond of (and pleased by) devotion.

119. Om bhakti gamyāyai namaḥ

...who is attained only through devotion.

120. Om bhakti vaśyāyai namaḥ

...who is to be won over by devotion.

121. Om bhayāpahāyai namaḥ

...who dispels fear.

122. Om śāmbhavyai namaḥ

...who is the wife of Sambhu (Shiva).

123. Om śāradārādhyāyai namaḥ

...who is worshipped by Sarada (Sarasvati, the Goddess of Speech).

124. Om śarvāṇyai namaḥ

...who is the wife of Sarva (Shiva).

125. Om śarma dāyinyai namaḥ

...who confers happiness.

126. Om śāṅkaryai namaḥ

...who gives happiness.

127. Om śrīkaryai namaḥ

...who bestows riches in abundance.

128. Om sādhvyai namaḥ

...who is chaste.

129. Om śarac candra nibhānanāyai namaḥ

...whose face shines like the full moon in the clear autumn sky.

130. Om śātodaryai namaḥ

...who is slender waisted.

131. Om śāntimatyai namaḥ

...who is peaceful.

132. Om nir ādhārāyai namaḥ

...who is without dependence.

133. Om nir añjanāyai namaḥ

...who stays unattached, bound to nothing.

134. Om nir lepāyai namaḥ

...who is free from all impurities arising from action.

135. Om nir malāyai namaḥ

...who is free from all impurities.

136. Om nityāyai namaḥ

...who is eternal.

137. Om nir ākārāyai namaḥ

...who is without form.

138. Om nir ākulāyai namaḥ

...who is without agitation.

139. Om nir guṇāyai namaḥ

...who is beyond all three gunas of nature, namely sattva, rajas and tamas.

140. Om niṣ kalāyai namaḥ

...who is without parts.

141. Om śāntāyai namaḥ

...who is tranquil.

142. Om niṣ kāmāyai namaḥ

...who is without desire.

143. Om nir upaplavāyai namaḥ

...who is indestructible.

144. Om nitya muktāyai namaḥ
...who is ever free from worldly bonds.

145. Om nir vikārāyai namaḥ
...who is unchanging.

146. Om niṣ prapañcāyai namaḥ
...who is not of this universe.

147. Om nir āśrayāyai namaḥ
...who does not depend on anything.

148. Om nitya śuddhāyai namaḥ
...who is eternally pure.

149. Om nitya buddhāyai namaḥ
...who is ever wise.

150. Om nir avadyāyai namaḥ
...who is blameless or praiseworthy.

151. Om nir antarāyai namaḥ
...who is all pervading.

152. Om niṣ kāraṇāyai namaḥ
...who is without cause.

153. Om niṣ kalaṅkāyai namaḥ
...who is faultless.

154. Om nir upādhaye namaḥ
...who is not conditioned or has no limitations.

155. Om nir īśvarāyai namaḥ
...who has no superior or protector.

156. Om nīrāgāyai namaḥ
...who has no desire.

157. Om rāga mathanāyai namaḥ
...who destroys desires (passions).

158. Om nir madāyai namaḥ
...who is without pride.

159. Om mada nāśinyai namaḥ
...who destroys pride.

160. Om niś cintāyai namaḥ
...who has no anxiety in anything.

161. Om nir ahaṅkārāyai namaḥ
...who is without egoism (without the concept of 'I' and 'mine').

162. Om nir mohāyai namaḥ
...who is free from delusion.

163. Om moha nāśinyai namaḥ
...who destroys delusion in Her devotees.

164. Om nir mamāyai namaḥ
...who has no self interest in anything.

165. Om mamatā hantryai namaḥ
...who destroys the sense of ownership.

166. Om niṣ pāpāyai namaḥ
...who is without sin.

167. Om pāpa nāśinyai namaḥ
...who destroys all the sins of Her devotees.

168. Om niṣ krodhāyai namaḥ
...who is without anger.

169. Om krodha śamanyai namaḥ
...who destroys anger in Her devotees.

170. Om nir lobhāyai namaḥ
...who is without greed.

171. Om lobha nāśinyai namaḥ
...who destroys greed in Her devotees.

172. Om niḥ saṁśayāyai namaḥ

...who is without doubts.

173. Om saṁśaya ghnyai namaḥ

...who kills all doubts.

174. Om nir bhavāyai namaḥ

...who is without origin.

175. Om bhava nāśinyai namaḥ

...who destroys the sorrow of samsara (the cycle of birth and death).

176. Om nir vikalpāyai namaḥ

...who is free of false imaginings.

177. Om nir ābādhāyai namaḥ

...who is not disturbed by anything.

178. Om nir bhedāyai namaḥ

...who is beyond all sense of difference.

179. Om bheda nāśinyai namaḥ

...who removes from Her devotees all sense of differences born of vasanas.

180. Om nir nāśāyai namaḥ

...who is imperishable.

181. Om mṛtyu mathanyai namaḥ

...who destroys death.

182. Om niṣ kriyāyai namaḥ

...who remains without action.

183. Om niṣ parigrahāyai namaḥ

...who does not acquire or accept anything.

184. Om nis tulāyai namaḥ

...who is incomparable, unequalled.

185. Om nīla cikurāyai namaḥ

...who has shining black hair.

186. Om nir apāyāyai namaḥ

...who is imperishable.

187. Om nir atyayāyai namaḥ

...who cannot be transgressed.

188. Om durlabhāyai namaḥ

...who is won only with much difficulty.

189. Om durgamāyai namaḥ

...who is approachable only with extreme effort.

190. Om durgāyai namaḥ

...who is the Goddess Durga.

191. Om duḥkha hantryai namaḥ

...who is the destroyer of sorrow.

192. Om sukha pradāyai namaḥ

...who is the giver of happiness.

193. Om duṣṭa dūrāyai namaḥ
...who is distant from those who are wicked.

194. Om durācāra śamanyai namaḥ
...who stops evil customs.

195. Om doṣa varjitāyai namaḥ
...who is free from all faults.

196. Om sarvajñāyai namaḥ
...who is omniscient.

197. Om sāndra karuṇāyai namaḥ
...who shows intense compassion.

198. Om samānādhika varjitāyai namaḥ
...who has neither equal nor superior.

199. Om sarva śakti mayyai namaḥ
...who has all the divine powers.

200. Om sarva maṅgalāyai namaḥ

...who is the source of all that is auspicious.

201. Om sad gati pradāyai namaḥ

...who leads into the right path.

202. Om sarveśvaryai namaḥ

...who rules over all the living and nonliving things.

203. Om sarva mayyai namaḥ

...who pervades every living and nonliving thing.

204. Om sarva mantra svarūpiṇyai namaḥ

...who is the essence of all the mantras.

205. Om sarva yantrātmikāyai namaḥ

...who is the soul of all yantras.

206. Om sarva tantra rūpāyai namaḥ

...who is the soul of all the tantras.

207. Om manonmanyai namaḥ
...who is Shiva's shakti.

208. Om māheśvaryai namaḥ
...who is the wife of Maheshvara.

209. Om mahā devyai namaḥ
...who has the immeasurable body.

210. Om mahā lakṣmyai namaḥ
...who is the great Goddess Lakshmi.

211. Om mṛḍa priyāyai namaḥ
...who is the beloved of Mrida (Shiva).

212. Om mahā rūpāyai namaḥ
...who has a great form.

213. Om mahā pūjyāyai namaḥ
...who is the greatest object of worship.

214. Om mahā pātaka nāśinyai namaḥ
...who destroys even the greatest of sins.

215. Om mahā māyāyai namaḥ
...who is the Great Illusion.

216. Om mahā sattvāyai namaḥ
...who possesses great sattva.

217. Om mahā śaktyai namaḥ
...who has great power.

218. Om mahā ratyai namaḥ
...who is boundless delight.

219. Om mahā bhogāyai namaḥ
...who has immense wealth.

220. Om mahaiśvaryāyai namaḥ
...who has supreme sovereignty.

221. Om mahā vīryāyai namaḥ

...who is supreme in valor.

222. Om mahā balāyai namaḥ

...who is supreme in might.

223. Om mahā buddhyai namaḥ

...who is supreme in intelligence.

224. Om mahā siddhyai namaḥ

...who is endowed with the highest attainments.

225. Om mahā yogeśvareśvaryai namaḥ

...who is the object of worship even by the greatest of yogis.

226. Om mahā tantrāyai namaḥ

...who is worshipped by the great tantras such as Kularnava and Jnanarnava.

227. Om mahā mantrāyai namaḥ

...who is the greatest mantra.

228. Om mahā yantrāyai namaḥ

...who is in the form of the great yantras.

229. Om mahāsanāyai namaḥ

...who is seated on great seats.

230. Om mahā yāga kramārādhyāyai namaḥ

...who is worshipped by the ritual of mahayaga.

231. Om mahā bhairava pūjitāyai namaḥ

...who is worshipped even by Mahabhairava (Shiva).

232. Om maheśvara mahākalpa mahātāṇḍava sākṣiṇyai namaḥ

...who is the witness of the great Tandava dance of Maheshvara (Shiva) at the end of the great cycle of creation.

233. Om mahā kāmeśa mahiṣyai namaḥ

...who is the great Queen of Mahakameshvara.

234. Om mahā tripura sundaryai namaḥ

...who is the great Tripurasundari.

235. Om catuḥ ṣaṣtyupacārāḍhyāyai namaḥ

...who is adored in sixty four ceremonies.

236. Om catuḥ ṣaṣṭi kalā mayyai namaḥ

...who embodies the sixty four fine arts.

237. Om mahā catuḥ ṣaṣṭi koṭi yoginī gaṇa sevitāyai namaḥ

...who is attended by six hundred forty million yoginis.

238. Om manu vidyāyai namaḥ

...who is the embodiment of Manuvidya.

239. Om candra vidyāyai namaḥ

...who is the embodiment of Candravidya.

240. Om candra maṇḍala madhyagāyai namaḥ

...who resides in the center of candramandala, the moon's disc.

241. Om cāru rūpāyai namaḥ

...who has a beauty that does not wax or wane.

242. Om cāru hāsāyai namaḥ

...who has a beautiful smile.

243. Om cāru candra kalā dharāyai namaḥ

...who wears a beautiful crescent moon that does not wax or wane.

244. Om carācara jagan nāthāyai namaḥ

...who is the ruler of the animate and inanimate worlds.

245. Om cakra rāja niketanāyai namaḥ

...who abides in the Sri Chakra.

246. Om pārvatyai namaḥ

...who is the daughter of the Mountain (Mount Himavat or Himalaya).

247. Om padma nayanāyai namaḥ

...who has eyes that are long and beautiful like the petals of the lotus flower.

248. Om padma rāga sama prabhāyai namaḥ

...who has a resplendent red complexion like the ruby.

249. Om pañca pretāsanāsīnāyai namaḥ
...who sits on the seat formed by five corpses.

250. Om pañca brahma svarūpiṇyai namaḥ
...whose form is composed of the five Brahmas.

251. Om cinmayyai namaḥ
...who is consciousness itself.

252. Om paramānandāyai namaḥ
...who is supreme bliss.

253. Om vijñāna ghana rūpiṇyai namaḥ
...who is the embodiment of all pervading solid Intelligence.

254. Om dhyāna dhyātṛ dhyeya rūpāyai namaḥ
...who shines as meditation, meditator and the object of meditation.

255. Om dharmādharma vivarjitāyai namaḥ
...who is devoid of (transcends) both virtue and vice.

256. Om viśva rūpāyai namaḥ
...who has the whole universe as Her form.

257. Om jāgariṇyai namaḥ
...who assumes the form of the jiva who is in the waking state.

258. Om svapantyai namaḥ
...who assumes the form of the jiva in the dream state.

259. Om taijasātmikāyai namaḥ
...who is the soul of the jiva in the dream state.

260. Om suptāyai namaḥ
...who assumes the form of the jiva experiencing deep sleep.

261. Om prājñātmikāyai namaḥ
...who is not separate from the jiva in the state of deep sleep.

262. Om turyāyai namaḥ
...who is in the state of turya, the fourth state.

263. Om sarvāvasthā vivarjitāyai namaḥ
...who transcends all states.

264. Om sṛṣṭi kartryai namaḥ
...who is the Creator.

265. Om brahma rūpāyai namaḥ
...who is in the form of Brahma for the creation of the universe.

266. Om goptryai namaḥ
...who protects.

267. Om govinda rūpiṇyai namaḥ
...who is in the form of Govinda (Vishnu) for the preservation of the universe.

268. Om saṁhāriṇyai namaḥ
...who is the destroyer of the universe.

269. Om rudra rūpāyai namaḥ
...who is in the form of Rudra (Shiva) for the dissolution of the universe.

270. Om tirodhāna karyai namaḥ

...who causes the disappearance of things.

271. Om īśvaryai namaḥ

...who protects and rules everything.

272. Om sadā śivāyai namaḥ

...who as Sadashiva always bestows auspiciousness.

273. Om anugraha dāyai namaḥ

...who confers blessing.

274. Om pañca kṛtya parāyaṇāyai namaḥ

...who is devoted to the five functions (mentioned in the mantras above).

275. Om bhānu maṇḍala madhyasthāyai namaḥ

...who abides at the center of the sun's disc.

276. Om bhairavyai namaḥ

...who is the wife of Bhairava (Shiva).

277. Om bhaga mālinyai namaḥ

...who wears a garland made of the six excellences.

278. Om padmāsanāyai namaḥ

...who is seated in the lotus flower.

279. Om bhagavatyai namaḥ

...who protects those who worship Her.

280. Om padma nābha sahodaryai namaḥ

...who is Lotus Navel's (Visnu's) sister.

281. Om unmeṣa nimiṣotpanna vipanna bhuvanāvalyai namaḥ

...who causes a series of worlds to arise and disappear with the opening and closing of Her eyes.

282. Om sahasra śīrṣa vadanāyai namaḥ

...who has a thousand heads and faces.

283. Om sahasrākṣyai namaḥ

...who has a thousand eyes.

284. Om sahasra pade namaḥ

...who has a thousand feet.

285. Om ābrahma kīṭa jananyai namaḥ

...who is the mother of everything from Brahma to the lowliest insect.

286. Om varṇāśrama vidhāyinyai namaḥ

...who established the order of the social division in life.

287. Om nijājñā rūpa nigamāyai namaḥ

...whose commands take the form of the Vedas.

288. Om puṇyāpuṇya phala pradāyai namaḥ

...who dispenses the fruits of both good and evil actions.

289. Om śruti sīmanta sindūrī kṛta pādābja dhūlikāyai namaḥ

...the dust from whose feet forms the vermillion marks at the parting line of the hair of the Sruti devatas (Vedas personified as goddesses).

290. Om sakalāgama sandoha śukti sampuṭa mauktikāyai namaḥ

...who is the pearl enclosed in the shell made of all the scriptures.

291. Om puruṣārtha pradāyai namaḥ
...who grants the (four fold) objects of human life.

292. Om pūrṇāyai namaḥ
...who is always whole, without growth or decay.

293. Om bhoginyai namaḥ
...who is the enjoyer.

294. Om bhuvaneśvaryai namaḥ
...who is the ruler of the universe.

295. Om ambikāyai namaḥ
...who is the Mother of the universe.

296. Om anādi nidhanāyai namaḥ
...who has neither beginning nor end.

297. Om hari brahmendra sevitāyai namaḥ
...who is attended by Vishnu, Brahma, and Indra.

298. Om nārāyaṇyai namaḥ
...who is the female counterpart of Narayana.

299. Om nāda rūpāyai namaḥ
...who is in the form of sound.

300. Om nāma rūpa vivarjitāyai namaḥ
...who has no name or form.

301. Om hrīṅ kāryai namaḥ
...who is in the form of the syllable hrim.

302. Om hrīmatyai namaḥ
...who is endowed with modesty.

303. Om hṛdyāyai namaḥ
...who abides in the heart.

304. Om heyopādeya varjitāyai namaḥ
...who has nothing to reject or accept.

305. Om rāja rājārcitāyai namaḥ

...who is worshipped by the king of kings.

306. Om rājñyai namaḥ

...who is the Queen of Shiva, the Lord of all kings.

307. Om ramyāyai namaḥ

...who gives delight, who is lovely.

308. Om rājīva locanāyai namaḥ

...whose eyes are like lotus, deer and fish.

309. Om rañjinyai namaḥ

...who delights the mind.

310. Om ramaṇyai namaḥ

...who gives joy.

311. Om rasyāyai namaḥ

...who is to be enjoyed; who enjoys.

312. Om raṇat kiṅkiṇi mekhalāyai namaḥ

...who wears a girdle of tinkling bells.

313. Om ramāyai namaḥ

...who has become Lakshmi and Sarasvati.

314. Om rākendu vadanāyai namaḥ

...who has a delightful face like the full moon.

315. Om rati rūpāyai namaḥ

...who is in the form of Rati, the wife of Kama.

316. Om rati priyāyai namaḥ

...who is fond of Rati; who is served by Rati.

317. Om rakṣā karyai namaḥ

...who is the protector.

318. Om rākṣasa ghnyai namaḥ

...who is the slayer of the entire race of demons.

319. Om rāmāyai namaḥ

...who gives delight.

320. Om ramaṇa lampaṭāyai namaḥ

...who is devoted to the Lord of Her heart, Lord Shiva.

321. Om kāmyāyai namaḥ

..who is to be desired.

322. Om kāma kalā rūpāyai namaḥ

...who is in the form of Kamakala.

323. Om kadamba kusuma priyāyai namaḥ

...who is especially fond of kadamba flowers.

324. Om kalyāṇyai namaḥ

...who bestows auspiciousness.

325. Om jagatī kandāyai namaḥ

...who is the root of the whole world.

326. Om karuṇā rasa sāgarāyai namaḥ

...who is the ocean of compassion.

327. Om kalāvatyai namaḥ

...who is the embodiment of all arts.

328. Om kalālāpāyai namaḥ

...who speaks musically and sweetly.

329. Om kāntāyai namaḥ

...who is beautiful.

330. Om kādambarī priyāyai namaḥ

...who is fond of mead.

331. Om varadāyai namaḥ

...who grants boons generously.

332. Om vāma nayanāyai namaḥ

...who has beautiful eyes.

333. Om vāruṇī mada vihvalāyai namaḥ

...who is intoxicated by varuni (liquor, soma, or bliss).

334. Om viśvādhikāyai namaḥ

...who transcends the universe.

335. Om veda vedyāyai namaḥ

...who is known through the Vedas.

336. Om vindhyācala nivāsinyai namaḥ

...who resides in the Vindhya mountains.

337. Om vidhātryai namaḥ

...who creates and sustains this universe.

338. Om veda jananyai namaḥ

...who is the Mother of the Vedas.

339. Om viṣṇu māyāyai namaḥ

...who is the illusory power of Vishnu.

340. Om vilāsinyai namaḥ

...who is playful.

341. Om kṣetra svarūpāyai namaḥ

...whose body is matter.

342. Om kṣetreśyai namaḥ

...who is the wife of Shiva, the Lord of matter and the body of all beings

343. Om kṣetra kṣetrajña pālinyai namaḥ

...who is the protector and knower of matter, thus the protector of body and soul.

344. Om kṣaya vṛddhi vinirmuktāyai namaḥ

...who is free from growth and decay.

345. Om kṣetra pāla samarcitāyai namaḥ

...who is worshipped by Ksetrapala.

346. Om vijayāyai namaḥ

...who is ever victorious.

347. Om vimalāyai namaḥ

...who is without a trace of impurity.

348. Om vandyāyai namaḥ

...who is adorable, worthy of worship.

349. Om vandāru jana vatsalāyai namaḥ

...who is full of motherly love for those who worship Her.

350. Om vāg vādinyai namaḥ

...who speaks.

351. Om vāma keśyai namaḥ

...who has beautiful hair.

352. Om vahni maṇḍala vāsinyai namaḥ

...who resides in the disc of fire.

353. Om bhaktimat kalpa latikāyai namaḥ

...who is the kalpa creeper to Her devotees.

354. Om paśu pāśa vimocinyai namaḥ

...who releases the ignorant from bondage.

355. Om saṁhṛtāśeṣa pāṣaṇḍāyai namaḥ

...who destroys all heretics.

356. Om sadācāra pravartikāyai namaḥ

...who is immersed in (and inspires others to follow) right conduct.

357. Om tāpa trayāgni santapta samāhlādana candrikāyai namaḥ

...who is the moonlight that gives joy to those burned by the triple fire of misery.

358. Om taruṇyai namaḥ

...who is ever young.

359. Om tāpasārādhyāyai namaḥ

...who is worshipped by ascetics.

360. Om tanu madhyāyai namaḥ

...who has a slender waist.

361. Om tamopahāyai namaḥ

...who removes the ignorance born of tamas.

362. Om cityai namaḥ

...who is in the form of pure intelligence.

363. Om tat pada lakṣyārthāyai namaḥ

...who is the embodiment of Truth ('tat').

364. Om cid eka rasa rūpiṇyai namaḥ

...who is of the nature of pure intelligence, who is the cause of knowledge.

365. Om svātmānandalavī bhūta brahmādyānanda santatyai namaḥ

...whose bliss outshines the bliss of Brahma and others.

366. Om parāyai namaḥ

...who is the supreme; who transcends all.

367. Om pratyak citī rūpāyai namaḥ

...who is of the nature of unmanifested consciousness or Brahman.

368. Om paśyantyai namaḥ

...who is the second level of sound (after para, before madhyama and vaikari).

369. Om para devatāyai namaḥ

...who is the supreme deity; Parashakti.

370. Om madhyamāyai namaḥ

...who stays in the middle.

371. Om vaikharī rūpāyai namaḥ

...who is in the form of manifested sound.

372. Om bhakta mānasa haṁsikāyai namaḥ

...who is the swan in the minds of Her devotees.

373. Om kāmeśvara prāṇa nāḍyai namaḥ

...who is the very life of Kameshvara, Her consort.

374. Om kṛtajñāyai namaḥ

...who knows all of our actions as they occur.

375. Om kāma pūjitāyai namaḥ

...who is worshipped by Kama.

376. Om śṛṅgāra rasa sampūrṇāyai namaḥ

...who is filled with the essence of love.

377. Om jayāyai namaḥ

...who is victorious always and everywhere.

378. Om jālandhara sthitāyai namaḥ

...who resides in the Jalandhara pitha (Vishuddhi chakra).

379. Om oḍyāṇa pīṭha nilayāyai namaḥ

...whose abode is the center known as Odyana (Ajna chakra).

380. Om bindu maṇḍala vāsinyai namaḥ

...who resides in the bindu mandala.

381. Om raho yāga kramārādhyāyai namaḥ

...who is worshipped in secret through sacrificial rites.

382. Om rahas tarpaṇa tarpitāyai namaḥ

...who is to be gratified by the secret rites of worship.

383. Om sadyaḥ prasādinyai namaḥ

...who bestows Her grace immediately.

384. Om viśva sākṣiṇyai namaḥ

...who is witness to the whole universe.

385. Om sākṣi varjitāyai namaḥ

...who has no other witness.

386. Om ṣaḍ aṅga devatā yuktāyai namaḥ

...who is accompanied by the deities of the six parts.

387. Om ṣāḍ guṇya pari pūritāyai namaḥ

...who is fully endowed with the six good qualities.

388. Om nitya klinnāyai namaḥ

...who is ever compassionate.

389. Om nirupamāyai namaḥ

...who is incomparable.

390. Om nirvāṇa sukha dāyinyai namaḥ

...who confers the bliss of Liberation.

391. Om nityā ṣoḍaśikā rūpāyai namaḥ

...who is in the form of the sixteen daily deities.

392. Om śrīkaṇṭhārdha śarīriṇyai namaḥ

...who possesses half of the body of Srikantha (Shiva), who is in the form of ardhanarishvara (half female, half male god).

393. Om prabhāvatyai namaḥ

...who is effulgent.

394. Om prabhā rūpāyai namaḥ

...who is effulgence.

395. Om prasiddhāyai namaḥ

...who is celebrated.

396. Om parameśvaryai namaḥ

...who is the supreme sovereign.

397. Om mūla prakṛtyai namaḥ

...who is the first cause of the entire universe.

398. Om avyaktāyai namaḥ

...who is unmanifested.

399. Om vyaktāvyakta svarūpiṇyai namaḥ

...who is in the manifested and unmanifested forms.

400. Om vyāpinyai namaḥ

...who is all pervading.

401. Om vividhākārāyai namaḥ

...who has a multitude of forms.

402. Om vidyāvidyā svarūpiṇyai namaḥ

...who is in the form of both knowledge and ignorance.

403. Om mahā kāmeśa nayana kumudāhlāda kaumudyai namaḥ
...who is the moonlight gladdening the waterlilies that are Mahakamesha's eyes.

404. Om bhakta hārda tamo bheda bhānumad bhānu santatyai namaḥ
...who is the sunbeam which dispels the darkness from the heart of Her devotees.

405. Om śiva dūtyai namaḥ
...for whom Shiva is the messenger.

406. Om śivārādhyāyai namaḥ
...who is worshipped by Shiva.

407. Om śiva mūrtyai namaḥ
...whose form is Shiva Himself.

408. Om śivaṅkaryai namaḥ
...who confers prosperity (auspiciousness), who turns Her devotee into Shiva.

409. Om śiva priyāyai namaḥ
...who is beloved of Shiva.

410. Om śiva parāyai namaḥ

...who is solely devoted to Shiva.

411. Om śiṣṭeṣṭāyai namaḥ

...who is loved by the righteous, who loves righteous people.

412. Om śiṣṭa pūjitāyai namaḥ

...who is always worshipped by the righteous.

413. Om aprameyāyai namaḥ

...who is immeasurable by the senses.

414. Om svaprakāśāyai namaḥ

...who is self luminous.

415. Om mano vācām agocarāyai namaḥ

...who is beyond the range of mind and speech.

416. Om cicchaktyai namaḥ

...who is the power of consciousness.

417. Om cetanā rūpāyai namaḥ

...who is pure Consciousness.

418. Om jaḍa śaktyai namaḥ

...who is the maya that has transformed itself as the power of creation.

419. Om jaḍātmikāyai namaḥ

...who is in the form of the inanimate world.

420. Om gāyatryai namaḥ

...who is the Gayatri mantra.

421. Om vyāhṛtyai namaḥ

...who is of the nature of utterance, who presides over the power of speech.

422. Om sandyāyai namaḥ

...who is in the form of twilight.

423. Om dvija vṛnda niṣevitāyai namaḥ

...who is worshipped by the twice born.

424. Om tattvāsanāyai namaḥ
...who has tattvas as Her seat, who abides in tattva.

425. Om tasmai namaḥ
...who is meant by 'That,' the Supreme Truth, Brahman.

426. Om tubhyam namaḥ
...who is referred to by 'Thou.'

427. Om ayyai namaḥ
...the dear One.

428. Om pañca kośāntara sthitāyai namaḥ
...who resides within the five sheaths.

429. Om niḥsīma mahimne namaḥ
...whose glory is limitless.

430. Om nitya yauvanāyai namaḥ
...who is ever youthful.

431. Om mada śālinyai namaḥ

...who is shining in a state of inebriation or intoxication.

432. Om mada ghūrṇita raktākṣyai namaḥ

...whose eyes are reddened, rolling with rapture and inward looking.

433. Om mada pāṭala gaṇḍa bhuve namaḥ

...whose cheeks are rosy with rapture.

434. Om candana drava digdhāṅgyai namaḥ

...whose body is smeared with sandalwood paste.

435. Om cāmpeya kusuma priyāyai namaḥ

...who is especially fond of campaka flowers.

436. Om kuśalāyai namaḥ

...who is skillful.

437. Om komalākārāyai namaḥ

...who is graceful in form.

438. Om kurukullāyai namaḥ

...who is the shakti Kurukulla.

439. Om kuleśvaryai namaḥ

...who is the ruler of Kula (triad of the knower, the known, and knowledge).

440. Om kula kuṇḍālayāyai namaḥ

...who abides in Kulakunda (the center of Muladhara chakra).

441. Om kaula mārga tatpara sevitāyai namaḥ

...who is worshipped by those devoted to the Kaula tradition.

442. Om kumāra gaṇanāthāmbāyai namaḥ

...who is the mother of Subrahmania and Ganesha.

443. Om tuṣṭyai namaḥ

...who is ever content.

444. Om puṣṭyai namaḥ

...who is the power of nourishment.

445. Om matyai namaḥ

...who manifests as intelligence.

446. Om dhṛtyai namaḥ

...who is fortitude.

447. Om śāntyai namaḥ

...who is tranquility itself.

448. Om svasti matyai namaḥ

...who is the Ultimate Truth.

449. Om kāntyai namaḥ

...who is effulgence.

450. Om nandinyai namaḥ

...who gives delight.

451. Om vighna nāśinyai namaḥ

...who destroys all obstacles.

452. Om tejovatyai namaḥ
...who is effulgent.

453. Om tri nayanāyai namaḥ
...who has the sun, moon, and fire as Her three eyes.

454. Om lolākṣī kāma rūpiṇyai namaḥ
...who is in the form of love in women.

455. Om mālinyai namaḥ
...who is wearing garlands.

456. Om haṁsinyai namaḥ
...who is not separate from hamsas (accomplished yogins).

457. Om mātre namaḥ
...who is the Mother of the universe.

458. Om malayācala vāsinyai namaḥ
...who resides in the Malaya mountain.

459. Om sumukhyai namaḥ
...who has a beautiful face.

460. Om nalinyai namaḥ
...whose body is soft and beautiful like lotus petals.

461. Om subhruve namaḥ
...who has beautiful eyebrows.

462. Om śobhanāyai namaḥ
...who is always radiant.

463. Om suranāyikāyai namaḥ
...who is the leader of the gods.

464. Om kālakaṇṭhyai namaḥ
...who is the wife of dark throated Shiva.

465. Om kānti matyai namaḥ
...who is radiant.

466. Om kṣobhiṇyai namaḥ

...who creates upheaval in the mind.

467. Om sūkṣma rūpiṇyai namaḥ

...who has a form that is too subtle to be perceived by the sense organs.

468. Om vajreśvaryai namaḥ

...who is Vajreshvari, the sixth daily deity.

469. Om vāma devyai namaḥ

...who is the wife of Vamadeva (Shiva).

470. Om vayovasthā vivarjitāyai namaḥ

...who is exempt from changes due to age and time.

471. Om siddheśvaryai namaḥ

...who is the goddess worshipped by spiritual adepts.

472. Om siddha vidyāyai namaḥ

...who is in the form of the fifteen syllabled mantra.

473. Om siddha mātre namaḥ
...who is the mother of Siddhas.

474. Om yaśasvinyai namaḥ
...who is of unequalled renown.

475. Om viśuddhi cakra nilayāyai namaḥ
...who resides in the Visuddhi chakra.

476. Om ārakta varṇāyai namaḥ
...who is of slightly red (rosy) complexion.

477. Om tri locanāyai namaḥ
...who has three eyes.

478. Om khaṭvāṅgādi praharaṇāyai namaḥ
...who is armed with a club and other weapons.

479. Om vadanaika samanvitāyai namaḥ
...who possesses only one face.

480. Om pāyasānna priyāyai namaḥ
...who is especially fond of sweet rice.

481. Om tvaksthāyai namaḥ
...who is the deity of the organ of touch (skin).

482. Om paśu loka bhayaṅkaryai namaḥ
...who fills with fear the mortal beings bound by worldly existence.

483. Om amṛtādi mahāśakti saṁvṛtāyai namaḥ
...who is surrounded by Amrita and other shaktis.

484. Om ḍākinīśvaryai namaḥ
...who is the Dakini deity described by the nine preceding names.

485. Om anāhatābja nilayāyai namaḥ
...who resides in the anahata lotus in the heart.

486. Om śyāmābhāyai namaḥ
...who is black in complexion.

487. Om vadana dvayāyai namaḥ

...who has two faces.

488. Om daṁṣṭrojjvalāyai namaḥ

...who has shining tusks.

489. Om akṣa mālādi dharāyai namaḥ

...who is wearing garlands of rudraksa beads and other things.

490. Om rudhira saṁsthitāyai namaḥ

...who presides over the blood in the bodies of living beings.

491. Om kāla rātryādi śaktyaugha vṛtāyai namaḥ

...who is surrounded by Kalaratri and other shaktis.

492. Om snigdhaudana priyāyai namaḥ

...who is fond of food offerings containing ghee, oil, and other fats.

493. Om mahā vīrendra varadāyai namaḥ

...who bestows boons on great warriors.

494. Om rākiṇyambā svarūpiṇyai namaḥ

...who is in the form of Mother Rakini described in the nine previous names.

495. Om maṇipūrābja nilayāyai namaḥ

...who resides in the ten petaled lotus in the Manipuraka chakra.

496. Om vadana traya samyutāyai namaḥ

...who has three faces.

497. Om vajrādikāyudhopetāyai namaḥ

...who holds the vajra (lightning bolt) and other weapons.

498. Om ḍāmaryādibhir āvṛtāyai namaḥ

...who is surrounded by Damari and other attending deities.

499. Om rakta varṇāyai namaḥ

...who is red in complexion.

500. Om māṁsa niṣṭhāyai namaḥ

...who presides over the flesh in living beings.

501. Om guḍānna prīta mānasāyai namaḥ

...who is fond of sweet rice made with raw sugar.

502. Om samasta bhakta sukhadāyai namaḥ

...who confers happiness on all Her devotees.

503. Om lākinyambā svarūpiṇyai namaḥ

...who is in the form of Mother Lakini described in the previous eight names.

504. Om svādhiṣṭhānāmbuja gatāyai namaḥ

...who resides in the six petaled lotus in the Svadhisthana chakra.

505. Om catur vaktra manoharāyai namaḥ

...who has four beautiful faces.

506. Om śūlādyāyudha sampannāyai namaḥ

...who possesses the trident and other weapons (noose, skull and abhaya).

507. Om pīta varṇāyai namaḥ

...who is yellow in color.

508. Om ati garvitāyai namaḥ

...who is very proud (of Her weapons and Her captivating beauty).

509. Om medo niṣṭhāyai namaḥ

...who resides in the fat in living beings.

510. Om madhu prītāyai namaḥ

...who is fond of honey and other offerings made with honey.

511. Om bandhinyādi samanvitāyai namaḥ

...who is accompanied by Bandhini and other shaktis.

512. Om dadhyannāsakta hṛdayāyai namaḥ

...who is particularly fond of offerings made with curd.

513. Om kākinī rūpa dhāriṇyai namaḥ

...who is in the form of the Kakini yogini, described in the ten previous names.

514. Om mūlādhārāmbujārūḍhāyai namaḥ

...who is resident in the lotus in the Muladhara chakra.

515. Om pañca vaktrāyai namaḥ

...who has five faces.

516. Om asthi saṁsthitāyai namaḥ

...who resides in the bones.

517. Om aṅkuśādi praharaṇāyai namaḥ

...who holds the goad and other weapons.

518. Om varadādi niṣevitāyai namaḥ

...who is attended by Varada and other shaktis.

519. Om mudgaudanāsakta cittāyai namaḥ

...who is particularly fond of food offerings made of mung beans.

520. Om sākinyambā svarūpiṇyai namaḥ

...who is in the form of Mother Sakini described in the previous six names.

521. Om ājñā cakrābja nilayāyai namaḥ

...who resides in the two petaled lotus in the Ajna chakra.

522. Om śukla varṇāyai namaḥ

...who is white.

523. Om ṣaḍ ānanāyai namaḥ

...who has six faces.

524. Om majjā saṁsthāyai namaḥ

...who is the presiding deity of the bone marrow.

525. Om haṁsa vatī mukhya śakti samanvitāyai namaḥ

...who is accompanied by the shaktis Hamsavati and Kshamavati.

526. Om haridrānnaika rasikāyai namaḥ

...who is fond of food seasoned with turmeric.

527. Om hākinī rūpa dhāriṇyai namaḥ

...who is in the form of Hakini Devi described in the preceding six names.

528. Om sahasra dala padmasthāyai namaḥ

...who resides in the thousand petaled lotus.

529. Om sarva varṇopaśobhitāyai namaḥ

...who is radiant in many colors.

530. Om sarvāyudha dharāyai namaḥ

...who holds all the known weapons.

531. Om śukla saṁsthitāyai namaḥ

...who resides in the semen.

532. Om sarvatomukhyai namaḥ

...who has faces turned in all directions.

533. Om sarvaudana prīta cittāyai namaḥ

...who is pleased by all offerings of food.

534. Om yākinyambā svarūpiṇyai namaḥ

...who is in the form of the Yakini yogini (described in the six preceding names).

535. Om svāhāyai namaḥ

...who is the object of the invocation 'svaha' at the end of mantras chanted while offering oblations to the fire in yaga ceremonies.

536. Om svadhāyai namaḥ

...who is the object of the invocation 'svadha' at the end of mantras chanted while making offerings to the ancestors.

537. Om amatyai namaḥ

...who is in the form of ignorance or nescience.

538. Om medhāyai namaḥ

...who is in the form of wisdom (knowledge).

539. Om śrutyai namaḥ

...who is in the form of the Vedas.

540. Om smṛtyai namaḥ

...who is in the form of smrti.

541. Om anuttamāyai namaḥ

...who is the best, to Her who is not excelled by anyone.

542. Om puṇya kīrtyai namaḥ

...whose fame is sacred or righteous.

543. Om puṇya labhyāyai namaḥ

...who is attained only by righteous souls.

544. Om puṇya śravaṇa kīrtanāyai namaḥ

...who bestows merit on anyone who hears of Her and praises Her.

545. Om pulomajārcitāyai namaḥ

...who is worshipped by Indra's wife, Pulomaja.

546. Om bandha mocinyai namaḥ

...who is free from bonds; who gives release from bondage.

547. Om barbarālakāyai namaḥ

...who has wavy locks of hair.

548. Om vimarśa rūpiṇyai namaḥ

...who is in the form of Vimarsa.

549. Om vidyāyai namaḥ

...who is in the form of knowledge.

550. Om viyadādi jagat prasuve namaḥ

...who is the Mother of the universe, formed from ether and the other elements.

551. Om sarva vyādhi praśamanyai namaḥ

...who removes all diseases and sorrows.

552. Om sarva mṛtyu nivāriṇyai namaḥ

...who guards Her devotees from all kinds of death.

553. Om agra gaṇyāyai namaḥ

...who is to be considered the foremost.

554. Om acintya rūpāyai namaḥ

...who is of a form beyond the reach of thought.

555. Om kali kalmaṣa nāśinyai namaḥ

...who is the destroyer of the sins of the age of Kali.

556. Om kātyāyanyai namaḥ

...who is the daughter of a sage named Kata.

557. Om kāla hantryai namaḥ

...who is the destroyer of time (death).

558. Om kamalākṣa niṣevitāyai namaḥ

...in whom Vishnu takes refuge.

559. Om tāmbūla pūrita mukhyai namaḥ

...whose mouth is full from chewing betel.

560. Om dāḍimī kusuma prabhāyai namaḥ

...who shines like a pomegranate flower.

561. Om mṛgākṣyai namaḥ

...whose eyes are long and beautiful like those of a doe.

562. Om mohinyai namaḥ

...who is enchanting.

563. Om mukhyāyai namaḥ

...who is the first.

564. Om mṛḍānyai namaḥ

...who is the wife of Mrida (Shiva).

565. Om mitra rūpiṇyai namaḥ

...who is the friend of everyone, the friend of the universe.

566. Om nitya tṛptāyai namaḥ

...who is eternally contented.

567. Om bhakta nidhaye namaḥ

...who is the treasure of the devotees.

568. Om niyantryai namaḥ

...who controls and guides all beings on the right path.

569. Om nikhileśvaryai namaḥ

...who is the ruler of all.

570. Om maitryādi vāsanā labhyāyai namaḥ

...who is to be attained by love and other good dispositions.

571. Om mahā pralaya sākṣiṇyai namaḥ
...who is witness to the Great Dissolution.

572. Om parāśaktyai namaḥ
...who is the Original, Supreme Power.

573. Om parā niṣṭhāyai namaḥ
...who is the Supreme End, the supreme abidance.

574. Om prajñāna ghana rūpiṇyai namaḥ
...who is pure condensed knowledge.

575. Om mādhvī pānālasāyai namaḥ
...who is languid from drinking wine; who is not eager for anything.

576. Om mattāyai namaḥ
...who is intoxicated.

577. Om mātṛkā varṇa rūpiṇyai namaḥ
...who is in the form of the letters of the alphabet.

578. Om mahā kailāsa nilayāyai namaḥ
...who resides in the great Kailasa.

579. Om mṛṇāla mṛdu dor latāyai namaḥ
...whose arms are as soft and cool as the lotus stem.

580. Om mahanīyāyai namaḥ
...who is adorable.

581. Om dayā mūrtyai namaḥ
...who is the personification of compassion.

582. Om mahā sāmrājya śālinyai namaḥ
...who controls the great empire of the three worlds.

583. Om ātma vidyāyai namaḥ
...who is the knowledge of the Self.

584. Om mahā vidyāyai namaḥ
...who is the seat of exalted knowledge, the knowledge of the Self.

585. Om śrī vidyāyai namaḥ

...who is sacred knowledge.

586. Om kāma sevitāyai namaḥ

...who is worshipped by Kamadeva (the god of love).

587. Om śrī ṣoḍaśākṣarī vidyāyai namaḥ

...who is in the form of the sixteen syllabled mantra.

588. Om trikūṭāyai namaḥ

...who is in three parts.

589. Om kāma koṭikāyai namaḥ

...of whom Kama (Shiva) is a part or an approximate form.

590. Om kaṭākṣa kiṅkarī bhūta kamalā koṭi sevitāyai namaḥ

...who is attended by millions of Lakshmis who are subdued by Her mere glances.

591. Om śiraḥ sthitāyai namaḥ

...who resides in the head.

592. Om candra nibhāyai namaḥ

...who is resplendent like the moon.

593. Om bhālasthāyai namaḥ

...who resides in the forehead (between the eyebrows).

594. Om indra dhanuḥ prabhāyai namaḥ

...who is resplendent like the rainbow.

595. Om hṛdayasthāyai namaḥ

...who resides in the heart.

596. Om ravi prakhyāyai namaḥ

...who shines with the special brilliance of the sun.

597. Om trikoṇāntara dīpikāyai namaḥ

...who shines as a light within the triangle.

598. Om dākṣāyaṇyai namaḥ

...who is Satidevi, the daughter of Daksha Prajapati.

599. Om daitya hantryai namaḥ
...who is the killer of demons.

600. Om dakṣa yajña vināśinyai namaḥ
...who is the destroyer of the sacrifice conducted by Daksha.

601. Om darāndolita dīrghākṣyai namaḥ
...who has long, tremulous eyes.

602. Om dara hāsojjvalan mukhyai namaḥ
...whose face is radiant with a smile.

603. Om guru mūrtaye namaḥ
...who has assumed a severe form, who has assumed the form of the Guru.

604. Om guṇa nidhaye namaḥ
...who is the treasure house of all good qualities.

605. Om go mātre namaḥ
...who became Surabhi, the cow that grants all wishes.

606. Om guha janma bhuve namaḥ

...who is the Mother of Guha (Subrahmanya).

607. Om deveśyai namaḥ

...who is the protector of the gods.

608. Om daṇḍa nītisthāyai namaḥ

...who maintains the rules of justice without the slightest error.

609. Om daharākāśa rūpiṇyai namaḥ

...who is the subtle Self in the heart.

610. Om pratipan mukhya rākānta tithi maṇḍala pūjitāyai namaḥ

...who is worshipped daily starting with pratipad (first day of the lunar half month) and ending with the full moon.

611. Om kalātmikāyai namaḥ

...who is in the form of the kalas.

612. Om kalā nāthāyai namaḥ

...who is the mistress of all the kalas.

613. Om kāvyālāpa vinodinyai namaḥ

...who delights in hearing poetry.

614. Om sacāmara ramā vāṇī savya dakṣiṇa sevitāyai namaḥ

...who is attended by Lakshmi on the left side and Sarasvati on the right side, bearing ceremonial fans.

615. Om ādiśaktyai namaḥ

...who is the Primordial Power, the first shakti, the cause of the universe.

616. Om ameyāyai namaḥ

...who is not measurable by any means.

617. Om ātmane namaḥ

...who is the Self in all.

618. Om paramāyai namaḥ

...who is the Supreme.

619. Om pāvanākṛtaye namaḥ

...who is of sacred form.

620. Om aneka koṭi brahmāṇḍa jananyai namaḥ

...who is the creator of many millions of worlds.

621. Om divya vigrahāyai namaḥ

...who has a divine body.

622. Om klīṅkāryai namaḥ

...who is creator of the syllable klim.

623. Om kevalāyai namaḥ

...who is the absolute, who is complete, independent and without any attributes.

624. Om guhyāyai namaḥ

...who is to be known in secret.

625. Om kaivalya pada dāyinyai namaḥ

...who bestows Liberation.

626. Om tripurāyai namaḥ

...who is older than the Three.

627. Om trijagad vandyāyai namaḥ

...who is adored by the inhabitants of all three worlds.

628. Om tri mūrtyai namaḥ

...who is the aggregate of the Trinity (of Brahma, Vishnu, and Shiva).

629. Om tridaśeśvaryai namaḥ

...who is the ruler of the gods.

630. Om tryakṣaryai namaḥ

...whose form consists of three letters or syllables.

631. Om divya gandhāḍhyāyai namaḥ

...who is richly endowed with divine fragrance.

632. Om sindūra tilakāñcitāyai namaḥ

...who shines with a vermillion mark on Her forehead.

633. Om umāyai namaḥ

...who is Parvati Devi.

634. Om śailendra tanayāyai namaḥ

...who is the daughter of Himavat, the king of the mountains.

635. Om gauryai namaḥ

...who has a fair complexion.

636. Om gandharva sevitāyai namaḥ

...who is served by the gandharvas.

637. Om viśva garbhāyai namaḥ

...who contains the whole universe in Her womb.

638. Om svarṇa garbhāyai namaḥ

...who is the the cause of the universe.

639. Om avaradāyai namaḥ

...who destroys the unholy demons.

640. Om vāg adhīśvaryai namaḥ

...who presides over speech.

641. Om dhyāna gamyāyai namaḥ

...who is to be attained through meditation.

642. Om apari cchedyāyai namaḥ

...whose limits cannot be ascertained.

643. Om jñānadāyai namaḥ

...who gives knowledge of the Self.

644. Om jñāna vigrahāyai namaḥ

...who is the embodiment of Knowledge itself.

645. Om sarva vedānta saṁvedyāyai namaḥ

...who is known by all of Vedanta.

646. Om satyānanda svarūpiṇyai namaḥ

...whose form is existence and bliss.

647. Om lopāmudrārcitāyai namaḥ

...who is worshipped by Lopamudra, sage Agastya's wife.

648. Om līlā kḷpta brahmāṇḍa maṇḍalāyai namaḥ

...who has created and maintained the universe purely as a sport.

649. Om adṛśyāyai namaḥ

...who is not perceived by the sense organs.

650. Om dṛśya rahitāyai namaḥ

...who has nothing to see.

651. Om vijñātryai namaḥ

...who knows the truth of the physical universe.

652. Om vedya varjitāyai namaḥ

...who has nothing left to know.

653. Om yoginyai namaḥ

...who is constantly united with Parashiva; who possesses the power of yoga.

654. Om yogadāyai namaḥ

...who bestows the power of yoga.

655. Om yogyāyai namaḥ
...who deserves yoga of all kinds.

656. Om yogānandāyai namaḥ
...who is the bliss attained through yoga, who enjoys the bliss of yoga.

657. Om yugandharāyai namaḥ
...who is the Bearer of the yugas.

658. Om icchā śakti jñāna śakti kriyā śakti svarūpiṇyai namaḥ
...who is in the form of the powers of will, knowledge and action.

659. Om sarvādhārāyai namaḥ
...who is the support of all.

660. Om supratiṣṭhāyai namaḥ
...who is firmly established.

661. Om sad asad rūpa dhāriṇyai namaḥ
...who assumes the forms of both being and non being (sat and asat).

662. Om aṣṭa mūrtyai namaḥ

...who has eight forms.

663. Om ajā jaitryai namaḥ

...who conquers ignorance.

664. Om loka yātrā vidhāyinyai namaḥ

...who directs the course of the worlds.

665. Om ekākinyai namaḥ

...who is the lone one.

666. Om bhūma rūpāyai namaḥ

...who is the aggregate of all existing things.

667. Om nir dvaitāyai namaḥ

...who is without the sense of duality.

668. Om dvaita varjitāyai namaḥ

...who is beyond duality.

669. Om annadāyai namaḥ

...who is the giver of food to all living things.

670. Om vasudāyai namaḥ

...who is the giver of wealth.

671. Om vṛddhāyai namaḥ

...who is ancient.

672. Om brahmātmaikya svarūpiṇyai namaḥ

...whose nature is the union of Brahman and Atman.

673. Om bṛhatyai namaḥ

...who is immense.

674. Om brāhmaṇyai namaḥ

...who is predominantly sattvic.

675. Om brāhmyai namaḥ

...who presides over speech.

676. Om brahmānandāyai namaḥ

...who is ever immersed in the bliss of Brahman.

677. Om bali priyāyai namaḥ

...who is especially fond of sacrificial offerings.

678. Om bhāṣā rūpāyai namaḥ

...who is in the form of language.

679. Om bṛhat senāyai namaḥ

...who has a vast army.

680. Om bhāvābhāva vivarjitāyai namaḥ

...who is beyond being and non being.

681. Om sukhārādhyāyai namaḥ

...who is easily worshipped.

682. Om śubha karyai namaḥ

...who does good.

683. Om śobhanā sulabhā gatyai namaḥ

...who is attained through a bright and easy path.

684. Om rāja rājeśvaryai namaḥ

...who is the ruler of kings and emperors.

685. Om rājya dāyinyai namaḥ

...who gives dominion.

686. Om rājya vallabhāyai namaḥ

...who protects all the dominions.

687. Om rājat kṛpāyai namaḥ

...who has a compassion that captivates everyone.

688. Om rāja pīṭha niveśita nijāśritāyai namaḥ

...who establishes on royal thrones those who take refuge in Her.

689. Om rājya lakṣmyai namaḥ

...who is the embodiment of the prosperity of the world.

690. Om kośa nāthāyai namaḥ
...who is the Mistress of the Treasury.

691. Om catur aṅga baleśvaryai namaḥ
...who commands armies of four types.

692. Om sāmrājya dāyinyai namaḥ
...who is the bestower of imperial dominion.

693. Om satya sandhāyai namaḥ
...who is devoted to or maintains truth.

694. Om sāgara mekhalāyai namaḥ
...who is girdled by the oceans.

695. Om dīkṣitāyai namaḥ
...who is under a vow.

696. Om daitya śamanyai namaḥ
...who destroys the demons, wicked forces.

697. Om sarva loka vaśaṅkaryai namaḥ
...who keeps all the worlds under Her control.

698. Om sarvārtha dātryai namaḥ
...who grants all desires.

699. Om sāvitryai namaḥ
...who is the creative power in the universe.

700. Om sac cid ānanda rūpiṇyai namaḥ
...who is of the nature of existence, consciousness, and bliss.

701. Om deśa kālāparicchinnāyai namaḥ
...who is not limited (or measured) by time and space.

702. Om sarvagāyai namaḥ
...who pervades all the worlds and all the beings; who is omnipresent.

703. Om sarva mohinyai namaḥ
...who deludes all.

704. Om sarasvatyai namaḥ

...who is in the form of knowledge.

705. Om śāstramayyai namaḥ

...who is in the form of the scriptures; to Her whose limbs are the scriptures.

706. Om guhāmbāyai namaḥ

...who is the Mother of Subrahmanya, who dwells in the cave of the heart.

707. Om guhya rūpiṇyai namaḥ

...who has a secret form.

708. Om sarvopādhi vinirmuktāyai namaḥ

...who is free from all limitations.

709. Om sadāśiva pativratāyai namaḥ

...who is Sadashiva's devoted wife.

710. Om sampradāyeśvaryai namaḥ

...who is the guardian of sacred traditions.

711. Om sādhune namaḥ
...who possesses equanimity.

712. Om yai namaḥ
...who is the symbol I.

713. Om guru maṇḍala rūpiṇyai namaḥ
...who embodies in Herself the lineage of Gurus.

714. Om kulottīrṇāyai namaḥ
...who transcends the senses.

715. Om bhagārādhyāyai namaḥ
...who is worshipped in the sun's disc.

716. Om māyāyai namaḥ
...who is illusion.

717. Om madhumatyai namaḥ
...whose nature is as sweet as honey.

718. Om mahyai namaḥ

...who is the Goddess Earth.

719. Om gaṇāmbāyai namaḥ

...who is the mother of Shiva's attendants.

720. Om guhyakārādhyāyai namaḥ

...who is worshipped by guhyakas (kind of devas).

721. Om komalāṅgyai namaḥ

...who has beautiful limbs.

722. Om guru priyāyai namaḥ

...who is beloved of the gurus.

723. Om svatantrāyai namaḥ

...who is free from all limitations.

724. Om sarva tantreśyai namaḥ

...who is the goddess of all tantras.

725. Om dakṣiṇā mūrti rūpiṇyai namaḥ
...who is in the form of Dakshinamurti (Shiva, the original guru).

726. Om sanakādi samārādhyāyai namaḥ
...who is worshipped by Sanaka and other sages.

727. Om śiva jñāna pradāyinyai namaḥ
...who bestows the knowledge of Shiva.

728. Om cit kalāyai namaḥ
...who is the Consciousness in Brahman.

729. Om ānanda kalikāyai namaḥ
...who is the bud of bliss.

730. Om prema rūpāyai namaḥ
...who is pure love.

731. Om priyaṅkaryai namaḥ
...who grants what is dear to Her devotees.

732. Om nāma pārāyaṇa prītāyai namaḥ

...who is pleased by the repetition of Her names.

733. Om nandi vidyāyai namaḥ

...who is the deity worshipped by the mantra (vidya) of Nandi.

734. Om naṭeśvaryai namaḥ

...who is the wife of Natesha (Lord of Dance, Shiva).

735. Om mithyā jagad adhiṣṭhānāyai namaḥ

...who is the basis of the illusory universe.

736. Om mukti dāyai namaḥ

...who gives Liberation.

737. Om mukti rūpiṇyai namaḥ

...who is in the form of Liberation.

738. Om lāsya priyāyai namaḥ

...who is fond of the lasya dance.

739. Om laya karyai namaḥ
...who causes absorption.

740. Om lajjāyai namaḥ
...who exists as modesty in living beings.

741. Om rambhādi vanditāyai namaḥ
...who is adored by the celestial damsels such as Rambha.

742. Om bhava dāva sudhā vṛṣṭyai namaḥ
...who is the rain of nectar falling on the forest fire of worldly existence.

743. Om pāpāraṇya davānalāyai namaḥ
...who is like wild fire to the forest of sins.

744. Om daurbhāgya tūla vātūlāyai namaḥ
...who is the gale that drives away the cotton wisps of misfortune.

745. Om jarā dhvānta ravi prabhāyai namaḥ
...who is the sunlight that dispels the darkness of old age.

746. Om bhāgyābdhi candrikāyai namaḥ

...who is the full moon to the ocean of good fortune.

747. Om bhakta citta keki ghanāghanāyai namaḥ

...who is like the cloud that gladdens the peacocks for Her devotees' hearts.

748. Om roga parvata dambholaye namaḥ

...who is the thunderbolt that shatters the mountain of disease.

749. Om mṛtyu dāru kuṭhārikāyai namaḥ

...who is the axe that cuts down the tree of death.

750. Om maheśvaryai namaḥ

...who is the Supreme Goddess.

751. Om mahā kālyai namaḥ

...who is the great Kali.

752. Om mahā grāsāyai namaḥ

...who devours everything great or who is the great devourer.

753. Om mahāśanāyai namaḥ

...who eats everything that is great.

754. Om aparṇāyai namaḥ

...who owes no debt.

755. Om caṇḍikāyai namaḥ

...who is angry (at the wicked).

756. Om caṇḍa muṇḍāsura niṣūdinyai namaḥ

...who killed Canda, Munda and other asuras.

757. Om kṣarākṣarātmikāyai namaḥ

...who is in the form of both the perishable and imperishable Atman.

758. Om sarva lokeśyai namaḥ

...who is the ruler of all worlds.

759. Om viśva dhāriṇyai namaḥ

...who supports the universe.

760. Om tri varga dātryai namaḥ

...who bestows the three goals of life.

761. Om subhagāyai namaḥ

...who is the seat of all prosperity.

762. Om tryambakāyai namaḥ

...who has three eyes.

763. Om triguṇātmikāyai namaḥ

...who is the essence of the three gunas.

764. Om svargāpavargadāyai namaḥ

...who bestows heaven and liberation.

765. Om śuddhāyai namaḥ

...who is the purest.

766. Om japā puṣpa nibhākṛtyai namaḥ

...whose body is like the hibiscus flower.

767. Om ojovatyai namaḥ
...who is full of vitality.

768. Om dyuti dharāyai namaḥ
...who is full of light and splendor, who has an aura of light.

769. Om yajña rūpāyai namaḥ
...who is in the form of sacrifice.

770. Om priya vratāyai namaḥ
...who is fond of vows.

771. Om durārādhyāyai namaḥ
...who is difficult to worship.

772. Om durādharṣāyai namaḥ
...who is difficult to control.

773. Om pāṭalī kusuma priyāyai namaḥ
...who is fond of the patali flower (the pale red trumpet flower).

774. Om mahatyai namaḥ

...who is great.

775. Om meru nilayāyai namaḥ

...who resides in the Meru mountain.

776. Om mandāra kusuma priyāyai namaḥ

...who is fond of the mandara flowers.

777. Om vīrārādhyāyai namaḥ

...who is worshipped by heroic persons.

778. Om virāḍ rūpāyai namaḥ

...who is in the form of the Cosmic Whole.

779. Om virajase namaḥ

...who is without rajas.

780. Om viśvato mukhyai namaḥ

...who faces all directions.

781. Om pratyag rūpāyai namaḥ
...who is the indwelling Self.

782. Om parākāśāyai namaḥ
...who is the transcendental ether.

783. Om prāṇadāyai namaḥ
...who is the giver of life.

784. Om prāṇa rūpiṇyai namaḥ
...who is of the nature of life.

785. Om mārtāṇḍa bhairavārādhyāyai namaḥ
...who is worshipped by Martandabhairava.

786. Om mantriṇī nyasta rājya dhure namaḥ
...who has entrusted Her regal responsibilities to Her mantrini (minister).

787. Om tripureśyai namaḥ
...who is the Goddess of Tripura.

788. Om jayat senāyai namaḥ

...who has an army which is accustomed only to victory.

789. Om nistraiguṇyāyai namaḥ

...who is devoid of the three gunas.

790. Om parāparāyai namaḥ

...who is both para and apara.

791. Om satya jñānānanda rūpāyai namaḥ

...who is truth, knowledge and bliss.

792. Om sāmarasya parāyaṇāyai namaḥ

...who is immersed in a state of steady wisdom.

793. Om kapardinyai namaḥ

...who is the wife of Shiva (the one with matted hair).

794. Om kalā mālāyai namaḥ

...who wears all sixty four forms of art as a garland.

795. Om kāma dhuge namaḥ
...who fulfills all desires.

796. Om kāma rūpiṇyai namaḥ
...who has a desirable form.

797. Om kalā nidhaye namaḥ
...who is the treasure house of all arts.

798. Om kāvya kalāyai namaḥ
...who is the art of poetry.

799. Om rasa jñāyai namaḥ
...who knows all the rasas (sentiments).

800. Om rasa śevadhaye namaḥ
...who is the treasurehouse of rasa (bliss of Brahman).

801. Om puṣṭāyai namaḥ
...who is always full of vigor, nourishment.

802. Om purātanāyai namaḥ
...who is ancient.

803. Om pūjyāyai namaḥ
...who is worthy of worship by all.

804. Om puṣkarāyai namaḥ
...who is complete; to Her who gives nourishment to all.

805. Om puṣkarekṣaṇāyai namaḥ
...who has eyes like lotus petals.

806. Om parasmai jyotiṣe namaḥ
...who is the supreme light.

807. Om parasmai dhāmne namaḥ
...who is the supreme abode.

808. Om paramāṇave namaḥ
...who is the subtlest particle.

809. Om parāt parāyai namaḥ

...who is the most supreme of the supreme ones.

810. Om pāśa hastāyai namaḥ

...who holds a noose in Her hand.

811. Om pāśa hantryai namaḥ

...who destroys the bonds.

812. Om para mantra vibhedinyai namaḥ

...who breaks the spell of the evil mantras of the enemies.

813. Om mūrtāyai namaḥ

...who has forms.

814. Om amūrtāyai namaḥ

...who has no definite form.

815. Om anitya tṛptāyai namaḥ

...who is satisfied even by our perishable offerings.

816. Om muni mānasa haṁsikāyai namaḥ

...who is the swan in the Manasa lake of the mind of sages.

817. Om satya vratāyai namaḥ

...who abides firmly in truth.

818. Om satya rūpāyai namaḥ

...who is Truth itself.

819. Om sarvāntar yāmiṇyai namaḥ

...who dwells inside all.

820. Om satyai namaḥ

...who is Reality, the eternal Being.

821. Om brahmāṇyai namaḥ

...who is the tail that is Brahman; the support for all.

822. Om brahmaṇe namaḥ

...who is Brahman.

823. Om jananyai namaḥ

...who is the Mother.

824. Om bahu rūpāyai namaḥ

...who has a multitude of forms.

825. Om budhārcitāyai namaḥ

...who is worshipped by the wise.

826. Om prasavitryai namaḥ

...who is Mother of the Universe.

827. Om pracaṇḍāyai namaḥ

...who is full of awe inspiring wrath.

828. Om ājñāyai namaḥ

...who is divine commandment Herself.

829. Om pratiṣṭhāyai namaḥ

...who is the foundation.

830. Om prakaṭākṛtyai namaḥ
...who is manifested in the form of the universe.

831. Om prāṇeśvaryai namaḥ
...who lords over the five pranas and the senses.

832. Om prāṇa dātryai namaḥ
...who is the giver of life.

833. Om pañcāśat pīṭha rūpiṇyai namaḥ
...who has fifty centers of worship.

834. Om viśṛṅkhalāyai namaḥ
...who is unfettered, free in every way.

835. Om viviktasthāyai namaḥ
...who abides in secluded places.

836. Om vīra mātre namaḥ
...who is the Mother of the valiant; Mother to the best among the devotees.

837. Om viyat prasuve namaḥ

...who is Mother to the ether.

838. Om mukundāyai namaḥ

...who gives salvation.

839. Om mukti nilayāyai namaḥ

...who is the abode of salvation.

840. Om mūla vigraha rūpiṇyai namaḥ

...who is the root form of everything.

841. Om bhāva jñāyai namaḥ

...who is the knower of all thoughts and sentiments.

842. Om bhava roga ghnyai namaḥ

...who eradicates the diseases of the cycle of birth and death.

843. Om bhava cakra pravartinyai namaḥ

...who turns the wheel of the cycle of birth and death.

844. Om chandaḥ sārāyai namaḥ

...who is the essence of all the Vedas.

845. Om śāstra sārāyai namaḥ

...who is the essence of all scriptures.

846. Om mantra sārāyai namaḥ

...who is the essence of all mantras.

847. Om talodaryai namaḥ

...who has a slim waist.

848. Om udāra kīrtaye namaḥ

...who possesses exalted fame.

849. Om uddāma vaibhavāyai namaḥ

...whose prowess is unlimited.

850. Om varṇa rūpiṇyai namaḥ

...who is in the form of the letters of the alphabet.

851. Om janma mṛtyu jarā tapta jana viśrānti dāyinyai namaḥ
...who gives peace and repose to those afflicted by birth, death, and decrepitude.

852. Om sarvopaniṣad udghuṣṭāyai namaḥ
...who is celebrated by all the Upanisads.

853. Om śāntyatīta kalātmikāyai namaḥ
...who transcends the state of peace.

854. Om gambhīrāyai namaḥ
...who is unfathomable.

855. Om gaganāntaḥsthāyai namaḥ
...who resides in the ether, space.

856. Om garvitāyai namaḥ
...who is proud.

857. Om gāna lolupāyai namaḥ
...who delights in music.

858. Om kalpanā rahitāyai namaḥ

...who is free from imaginary attributes.

859. Om kāṣṭhāyai namaḥ

...who dwells in the highest state (beyond which there is nothing).

860. Om akāntāyai namaḥ

...who ends all sins and sorrows.

861. Om kāntārdha vigrahāyai namaḥ

...who is half the body of Her husband.

862. Om kārya kāraṇa nirmuktāyai namaḥ

...who is free from the bond of cause and effect.

863. Om kāma keli taraṅgitāyai namaḥ

...who is overflowing with pleasure in the union with Kameshvara.

864. Om kanat kanaka tāṭaṅkāyai namaḥ

...who wears glittering gold ear ornaments.

865. Om līlā vigraha dhāriṇyai namaḥ
...who assumes various glorious forms as a sport.

866. Om ajāyai namaḥ
...who has no birth.

867. Om kṣaya vinirmuktāyai namaḥ
...who is free from decay.

868. Om mugdhāyai namaḥ
...who is captivating in Her beauty.

869. Om kṣipra prasādinyai namaḥ
...who is quickly pleased.

870. Om antar mukha samārādhyāyai namaḥ
...who is to be worshipped internally (by mental worship).

871. Om bahir mukha sudurlabhāyai namaḥ
...who is difficult to attain by those whose attention is directed outwards.

872. Om trayyai namaḥ

...who is the three Vedas.

873. Om trivarga nilayāyai namaḥ

...who is the abode of the threefold aims of human life.

874. Om tristhāyai namaḥ

...who resides in the three worlds.

875. Om tripura mālinyai namaḥ

...who is Tripuramalini (a Goddess in the Sri Chakra).

876. Om nir āmayāyai namaḥ

...who is free from diseases of all kinds.

877. Om nir ālambāyai namaḥ

...who depends on none.

878. Om svātmārāmāyai namaḥ

...who rejoices in Her own Self.

879. Om sudhāsṛtyai namaḥ

...who is the source of nectar.

880. Om saṁsāra paṅka nirmagna samuddharaṇa paṇḍitāyai namaḥ

...who is skilled in raising those immersed in the mire of transmigratory life.

881. Om yajña priyāyai namaḥ

...who is fond of sacrifices and other rituals.

882. Om yajña kartryai namaḥ

...who is the doer of sacrificial rites.

883. Om yajamāna svarūpiṇyai namaḥ

...who is in the form of Yajamana, who directs sacrificial rites.

884. Om dharmādhārāyai namaḥ

...who is the support of the code for righteous living.

885. Om dhanādhyakṣāyai namaḥ

...who oversees wealth.

886. Om dhana dhānya vivardhinyai namaḥ

...who increases wealth and harvests.

887. Om vipra priyāyai namaḥ

...who is fond of the learned.

888. Om vipra rūpāyai namaḥ

...who is in the form of a knower of the Self.

889. Om viśva bhramaṇa kāriṇyai namaḥ

...who makes the universe go around through Her power of illusion.

890. Om viśva grāsāyai namaḥ

...who devours the universe.

891. Om vidrumābhāyai namaḥ

...who shines like coral (with Her red complexion).

892. Om vaiṣṇavyai namaḥ

...who is in the form of Vishnu.

893. Om viṣṇu rūpiṇyai namaḥ

...who is in a form that extends over the whole universe.

894. Om ayonyai namaḥ

...who is without origin.

895. Om yoni nilayāyai namaḥ

...who is the seat of all origins.

896. Om kūṭasthāyai namaḥ

...who remains unchanged like the anvil.

897. Om kula rūpiṇyai namaḥ

...who is the deity of the Kaula path.

898. Om vīra goṣṭhī priyāyai namaḥ

...who is fond of the assembly of warriors.

899. Om vīrāyai namaḥ

...who is heroic.

900. Om naiṣkarmyāyai namaḥ
...who abstains from actions.

901. Om nāda rūpiṇyai namaḥ
...who is in the form of the primal sound.

902. Om vijñāna kalanāyai namaḥ
...who realizes the knowledge of Brahman.

903. Om kalyāyai namaḥ
...who is capable of creation.

904. Om vidagdhāyai namaḥ
...who is expert in everything.

905. Om baindavāsanāyai namaḥ
...who is seated in the Baindava (Ajna) chakra.

906. Om tattvādhikāyai namaḥ
...who transcends all cosmic categories.

907. Om tattva mayyai namaḥ

...who is Reality Itself or Shiva Himself.

908. Om tat tvam artha svarūpiṇyai namaḥ

...who is the meaning of tat (that) and tvam (you).

909. Om sāma gāna priyāyai namaḥ

...who is fond of the chanting of the Samaveda.

910. Om somyāyai namaḥ

...who is benign and gentle in nature; of a cool, gentle nature as the moon.

911. Om sadāśiva kuṭumbinyai namaḥ

...who is the wife of Sadashiva.

912. Om savyāpasavya mārgasthāyai namaḥ

...who occupies (or is reached by) both the left and the right paths of worship.

913. Om sarvāpad vinivāriṇyai namaḥ

...who removes all dangers.

914. Om svasthāyai namaḥ

...who abides in Herself; who is free from all afflictions.

915. Om svabhāva madhurāyai namaḥ

...who is sweet in Her inherent nature.

916. Om dhīrāyai namaḥ

...who is wise; who gives wisdom.

917. Om dhīra samarcitāyai namaḥ

...who is worshipped by the wise.

918. Om caitanyārghya samārādhyāyai namaḥ

...who is worshipped with consciousness as the oblation.

919. Om caitanya kusuma priyāyai namaḥ

...who is fond of the flower that is consciousness.

920. Om sadoditāyai namaḥ

...who is ever shining.

921. Om sadā tuṣṭāyai namaḥ
...who is ever pleased.

922. Om taruṇāditya pāṭalāyai namaḥ
...who is rosy like the morning sun.

923. Om dakṣiṇādakṣiṇārādhyāyai namaḥ
...who is adored by both right and left handed worshippers.

924. Om dara smera mukhāmbujāyai namaḥ
...whose lotus face holds a sweet smile.

925. Om kaulinī kevalāyai namaḥ
...who is worshipped as Pure Consciousness by those following the Kaula path.

926. Om anarghya kaivalya pada dāyinyai namaḥ
...who confers the priceless fruit of final Liberation.

927. Om stotra priyāyai namaḥ
...who is fond of hymns in Her praise.

928. Om stuti matyai namaḥ

...who is the true object, the essence, of all praises.

929. Om śruti saṁstuta vaibhavāyai namaḥ

...whose glory is celebrated in the srutis.

930. Om manasvinyai namaḥ

...who is well known for Her mind.

931. Om mānavatyai namaḥ

...who is high minded; who has great fame.

932. Om maheśyai namaḥ

...who is the wife of Shiva.

933. Om maṅgalākṛtaye namaḥ

...who is of auspicious form.

934. Om viśva mātre namaḥ

...who is the Mother of the Universe.

935. Om jagad dhātryai namaḥ
...who is the mother who protects and sustains the world.

936. Om viśālākṣyai namaḥ
...who has large eyes.

937. Om virāgiṇyai namaḥ
...who is dispassionate.

938. Om pragalbhāyai namaḥ
...who is skillful and confident.

939. Om paramodārāyai namaḥ
...who is supremely generous.

940. Om parā modāyai namaḥ
...who is supremely joyful.

941. Om manomayyai namaḥ
...who is in the form of the mind.

942. Om vyoma keśyai namaḥ

...who has the sky as Her hair.

943. Om vimānasthāyai namaḥ

...who is seated in Her celestial chariot.

944. Om vajriṇyai namaḥ

...who is the wife of Indra.

945. Om vāmakeśvaryai namaḥ

...who is the presiding deity of the Vamakesvara tantra.

946. Om pañca yajña priyāyai namaḥ

...who is fond of the five forms of sacrifices.

947. Om pañca preta mañcādhi śāyinyai namaḥ

...who reclines on a couch made of the Five Corpses.

948. Om pañcamyai namaḥ

...who is the fifth.

949. Om pañca bhūteśyai namaḥ

...who is the Goddess of the five elements.

950. Om pañca saṅkhyopacāriṇyai namaḥ

...who is worshipped using five objects of worship.

951. Om śāśvatyai namaḥ

...who is eternal.

952. Om śāśvataiśvaryāyai namaḥ

...who holds eternal sovereignty.

953. Om śarmadāyai namaḥ

...who is the giver of happiness.

954. Om śambhu mohinyai namaḥ

...who deludes Shiva.

955. Om dharāyai namaḥ

...who is Mother Earth.

956. Om dhara sutāyai namaḥ

...who is the daughter of Dhara (Himavat); Parvati.

957. Om dhanyāyai namaḥ

...who possesses great wealth, who is extremely blessed.

958. Om dharmiṇyai namaḥ

...who is righteous.

959. Om dharma vardhinyai namaḥ

...who promotes righteousness.

960. Om lokātītāyai namaḥ

...who transcends the worlds.

961. Om guṇātītāyai namaḥ

...who transcends the gunas.

962. Om sarvātītāyai namaḥ

...who transcends everything.

963. Om śamātmikāyai namaḥ

...who is of the nature of peace and bliss.

964. Om bandhūka kusuma prakhyāyai namaḥ

...who resembles the bandhuka flower in beauty and grace.

965. Om bālāyai namaḥ

...who never forsakes the nature of a child.

966. Om līlā vinodinyai namaḥ

...who delights in Her sport.

967. Om sumaṅgalyai namaḥ

...who is eternally auspicious, who never becomes a widow.

968. Om sukha karyai namaḥ

...who gives happiness.

969. Om suveṣāḍhyāyai namaḥ

...who is very attractive in Her beautiful rich garments and ornaments.

970. Om suvāsinyai namaḥ

...who is ever auspiciously married.

971. Om suvāsinyarcana prītāyai namaḥ

...who is pleased by the worship performed by married women.

972. Om āśobhanāyai namaḥ

...who is always radiant.

973. Om śuddha mānasāyai namaḥ

...who is of pure mind, who purifies the minds of Her worshippers.

974. Om bindu tarpaṇa santuṣṭāyai namaḥ

...who is pleased by offerings to the Bindu.

975. Om pūrva jāyai namaḥ

...who is ahead of everyone, who is first born.

976. Om tripurāmbikāyai namaḥ

...who is the Mother of the Three Cities.

977. Om daśa mudrā samārādhyāyai namaḥ
...who is worshipped by ten mudras.

978. Om tripurāśrī vaśaṅkaryai namaḥ
...for whom Tripurasri is under control.

979. Om jñāna mudrāyai namaḥ
...who is in the form of the jnana mudra (the finger pose of wisdom).

980. Om jñāna gamyāyai namaḥ
...who is to be attained through the yoga of knowledge.

981. Om jñāna jñeya svarūpiṇyai namaḥ
...who is both knowledge and the known.

982. Om yoni mudrāyai namaḥ
...who is in the form of the yoni mudra.

983. Om trikhaṇḍeśyai namaḥ
...who is the ruler of the tenth mudra, the trikhanda.

984. Om triguṇāyai namaḥ

...who is endowed with the three gunas.

985. Om ambāyai namaḥ

...who is Mother of all beings; Mother of the Universe.

986. Om trikoṇagāyai namaḥ

...who resides in the triangle.

987. Om anaghāyai namaḥ

...who is sinless.

988. Om adbhuta cāritrāyai namaḥ

...whose deeds are marvelous.

989. Om vāñchitārtha pradāyinyai namaḥ

...who gives all the desired objects.

990. Om abhyāsātiśaya jñātāyai namaḥ

...who is known only through the strenuous practice of spiritual discipline.

991. Om ṣaḍadhvātīta rūpiṇyai namaḥ
...whose form transcends the six paths.

992. Om avyāja karuṇā mūrtaye namaḥ
...who is pure compassion.

993. Om ajñāna dhvānta dīpikāyai namaḥ
...who is the bright lamp that dispels the darkness of ignorance.

994. Om ābāla gopa viditāyai namaḥ
...who is known well by all, even by children and cowherds.

995. Om sarvānullaṅghya śāsanāyai namaḥ
...whose commands are not disobeyed by anyone.

996. Om śrīcakra rāja nilayāyai namaḥ
...who abides in Sri Chakra, the king of chakras.

997. Om śrīmat tripura sundaryai namaḥ
...who is the divine Tripurasundari Devi.

998. Om śrī śivāyai namaḥ

...who is the auspicious and divine Shiva.

999. Om śiva śaktyaikya rūpiṇyai namaḥ

...who is the union of Shiva and Shakti into one form.

1000. Om lalitāmbikāyai namaḥ

...who is the Divine Mother Lalita (the playful one).

Mantrahīnam kriyāhīnam
bhaktihīnam maheśvari
yadpūjitam mayā devī
paripūrṇam tadastute

Oh Mother, in this worship of You, I may have forgotten to chant mantras, I may have forgotten to perform rituals, I may have done it without proper devotion or attention. Kindly forgive my omissions and make my worship full and complete, by your grace.

Śrī Mahiṣāsuramardini Stotram

Hymn to Her, who killed the buffalo demon

Ayi giri nandini nandita medini viśva vinodini nandanute
giri varavindya śirodhi nivāsini viṣṇu vilāsini jiṣṇunute
bhagavati he śitikaṇṭha kuṭumbini bhūri kuṭumbini bhūrikṛte
jaya jaya he mahiṣāsura-mardini ramyakapardini śailasute /1

Salutations, O Mother! You are a supreme delight to Your father (the Himalayas) as You have created the whole universe as if in a game. You are the happiness of all the beings in the creation. Your praises are sung even by Nandi (the vehicle of Shiva), You who reside on the lofty peaks of the great Vindhya mountain range. Vishnu derives his creative power only from You. Even the great god Indra prays to none other than Yourself. To You, the whole world is but one family.

Refrain:

Victory, Victory to the killer of the buffalo demon, the beloved of Shiva, the daughter of the mountain!

Suravara varṣiṇi durdhara dharṣiṇi durmukha marṣiṇi harṣarate
tribhuvana poṣiṇi śaṅkara toṣiṇi kalmaṣa moṣiṇi ghoṣarate
danu jani roṣiṇi ditisuta roṣiṇi durmada śoṣiṇi sindusute
jaya jaya he mahiṣāsura-mardini ramyakapardini śailasute /2

May victory be Yours, O Mother! You shower boons on all the gods. The giant Dhurdhara and the evil Durmukha were subdued by You. Established in imperishable bliss and delighting others You sustain the three worlds. You are the bliss of the great god Shiva. The war cries of the asuras were annihilated by You who were enraged by them. Of the evil-minded You are intolerant. To the egoistic Durmada You were the vehicle of death. You are the daughter of the ocean.

Ayi jagadamba madamba kadamba vana priya vāsini hāsarate
śikhari śiromaṇi tuṅgahimālaya śṛṅganijālaya madhyagate
madhu madhure madhukaiṭabha bhañjini kaiṭabha bhañjini rāsarate
jaya jaya he mahiṣāsura-mardini ramyakapardini śailasute /3

May victory be Yours, O Mother! You are my own Mother as well as the universal Mother of all of creation. The Kadamba forest is Your sacred dwelling place. You also abide on the majestic peaks of the Himalayan mountains. A pleasant smile, sweeter than honey, adorns Your beautiful face. The demons Madhu and Kaitabha were destroyed by You. You cleanse Your devotees of impurities and You rejoice in the divine rasa dance.

Ayi śata khaṇḍa vikhaṇḍita ruṇḍa vituṇḍita śuṇḍa gajādhipate
ripugaja gaṇḍa vidāraṇa caṇḍa parā krama śauṇḍa mṛgādhipate
nija bhujadaṇḍa nipātita caṇḍa vipātita muṇḍa bhaṭādhipate
jaya jaya he mahiṣāsura-mardini ramyakapardini śailasute /4

Glory to You, O Mother! With the weapon called Shatakhanda, You beheaded Your demonic enemies and cut them into hundreds of pieces. Your vehicle, the lion, destroyed the immense elephants of Your enemies while You destroyed the armies of the asuras with deadly blows from Your powerful hands.

Ayi raṇa durmada śatru vadhodita durdhara nirjara śaktibhṛte
catura vicāra dhurīṇa mahāśiva dūta kṛta pramathādhipate
durita durīha durāśaya durmati dānava dūta kṛtāntamate
jaya jaya he mahiṣāsura-mardini ramyakapardini śailasute /5

By annihilating the hordes of Demons, You reduced the heavy burden that had been carried by Mother Earth. You chose the introverted yogi, Shiva, as Your messenger to seek peace but, ultimately, You destroyed the insidious intentions of the asuras.

Ayi śaraṇāgata vairivadhūvara vīravarābhaya dāyikare
tribhu vana mastaka śūla virodhi śirodhi kṛtāmala śūlakare
dumi dumi tāmara dundubhināda mahomukharī kṛta diṅgikare
jaya jaya he mahiṣāsura-mardini ramyakapardini śailasute /6

Oh Mother! You granted boons to the wives of the asuras who sought refuge in You. Yet You were merciless to the other demons who remained a menace to creation, using Your trident to behead them. This act was praised by the gods who played on their drums and thus filled all of creation with the rhythmic sound of their instruments.

Ayi nija humkṛti mātra nirākṛta dhūmra vilocana dhūmraśate
sama ravi śoṣita śoṇita bīja samud bhava śoṇita bījalate
śiva śiva śumbha niśumbha mahāhava tarpita bhūta piśācapate
jaya jaya he mahiṣāsura-mardini ramyakapardini śailasute /7

O Mother! As if through a miracle the syllable 'Hum' which You loudly uttered reduced Dhumralochana and his evil allies to ashes. You destroyed Raktabija and his accomplices and You valiantly fought and killed Sumbha and Nisumbha. That act was pleasing to Shiva, the Lord of ghosts and ghouls.

Dhanu ranu ṣaṅga raṇakṣaṇa saṅga parisphura daṅga naṭatkaṭake
kanaka piśaṅga pṛṣatkaniṣaṅga rasad bhaṭaśṛṅga hatā baṭuke
kṛta catu raṅga balakṣiti raṅga ghaṭad bahuraṅga raṭad baṭuke
jaya jaya he mahiṣāsura-mardini ramyakapardini śailasute /8

O Mother! While wielding weapons in battle the bangles on Your hands jingled rhythmically. The bells tied to Your waistband shined and blinded Your enemies. Huge birds of prey hovered over the slain bodies of Your enemies who were scattered on the battle field.

Sura lalanā tatatho tatatho tatatho bhinayottara nṛtyarate
kṛta kukutho kukutho gaḍadādika tāla kutūhala gānarate
dhudhukuṭa dhukuṭa dhimdhimita dhvani dhīra mṛdaṅga ninādarate
jaya jaya he mahiṣāsura-mardini ramyakapardini śailasute /9

O Mother, the source of sound, You rejoice at the movements of celestial dancers who dance to the rhythm of the sounds 'tatato-tatato-tatato' and 'kukutha-kukutha-kukutha' and 'ga-ga-dha'.Their drum beats create the sounds 'kuthu-dhukuta-dhimi.'

Jaya jaya japya jaye jaya śabda parastuti tatpara viśvanute
jhaṇajhaṇa jhim jhimi jhimkṛta nūpura śiñjita mohita bhūtapate
naṭita naṭārdha naṭī naṭanāyaka nāṭita nāṭya sugānaratè
jaya jaya he mahiṣāsura-mardini ramyakapardini śailasute 10

Oh Mother! All of the devotees sing to You 'Victory! Victory!' You dance in union with Shiva during His tandava dance and He becomes pleased with the jingling sound that emanates from Your anklets.

Ayi sumunaḥ sumanaḥ sumanaḥ sumanaḥ sumanohara kāntiyute
śritarajanī rajanī rajanī rajanī rajanī kara vaktrayute
sunayana vibhramara bhramara bhramara bhramara bhramarādhipate
jaya jaya he mahiṣāsura-mardini ramyakapardini śailasute /11

Oh Mother! The Devas mentally offer You worship with flowers and Your captivating beauty assumes the from of the flower blossoms they visualize. Your face resembles a lotus that floats in a lake illuminated by the moon. The curls of Your hair toss like bees and add beauty to Your eyes.

Mahita mahāhava mallamatallika vallita rallaka bhallirate
viracita vallika pallika mallika jhillika bhillika vargavṛte
sitakṛta phulla samulla sitāruṇa tallaja pallava sallalite
jaya jaya he mahiṣāsura-mardini ramyakapardini śailasute /12

O Mother! When warriors unleash their weapons on a field of battle You watch over them. You are the refuge to the hill-dwellers and tribals that live in creeper bowers. When the twelve Adityas wait upon You then You shine even more brilliantly.

Avirala gaṇḍa galanmada medura matta mataṅgaja rājapate
tribhuvana bhūṣaṇa bhūta kalānidhi rūpa payonidhi rājasute
ayi sudatī jana lālasa mānasa mohana manmatha rājasute
jaya jaya he mahiṣāsura-mardini ramyakapardini śailasute /13

O Mother! Your majestic walk is like that of the king of the elephants from whose temple riches flowabundantly. You arose from the ocean as Maha Lakshmi along with the moon that adorns the three worlds. Manmatha, who infatuates young damsels, holds You in awe as he is powerless to enslave You with desire.

Kamala dalāmala komala kānti kalākalitāmala bhālalate
sakalavilāsa kalānilaya krama keli calat kalahaṁsakule
alikula saṅkula kuvalaya maṇḍala maulimilad-bakulālikule
jaya jaya he mahiṣāsura-mardini ramyakapardini śailasute /14

O Mother! Your beautiful forehead, which is broad and without match, excels the lotus petals in luster. Your graceful movements are like that of the swan. The Bakula flowers that adorn Your flowing hair attract swarms of bees.

Kala muralī rava vījitakūjita lajjita kokila mañjumate
milita pulinda manohara guñjita rañjita śaila nikuñjagate
nijaguṇa bhūta mahāśabarī gaṇa sad guṇa sambhṛta kelirate
jaya jaya he mahiṣāsura-mardini ramyakapardini śailasute /15

O Mother! The melodious notes emanating from Your flute cause the cuckoo to cease his song. In the Kalisha garden, You stand to watch the hunter women, Your devoted followers, and the bees hum sweetly.

Kaṭitaṭa pītadukūla vicitra mayūkha tiraskṛta candrarūce
praṇata surāsura mauli maṇisphura daṁśu lasannakha candraruce
jita kanakācala mauli madorjita nirbhara kuñjara kumbhakuce
jaya jaya he mahiṣāsura-mardini ramyakapardini śailasute /16

O Mother! The garment that You wear on Your slim waist excels the splendor of the moon. The nails on Your toes glow brightly and their radiance is enhanced by the crowns of both the suras and the asuras who prostrate in reverence before You. Your breasts are like the peaks of the Himalayas covered by waterfalls.

Vijita sahasra karaika sahasra karaika sahasra karaika nute
kṛta suratāraka saṅgaratāraka saṅgaratāraka sūnusute
suratha samādhi samāna samādhi samādhi samādhi sujātarate
jaya jaya he mahiṣāsura-mardini ramyakapardini śailasute /17

O Mother! The luster of the sun fades before You and he surrenders to You by pouring thousands of his rays at Your divine feet. The son of Tarakasura praises You profusely after the war. You delight to manifest in the mantra chanted with devotion by such devotees as Suratha and Samadhi in Saptasati.

Pada kamalam karuṇā nilaye vari vasyati yonudinam nuśive
ayi kamale kamalā nilaye kamalā nilayaḥ sa katham na bhavet
tava padameva param padamitya nuśīlayato mama kim na śive
jaya jaya he mahiṣāsura-mardini ramyakapardini śailasute /18

O Mother! Parvati! Worship performed for You grants one prosperity as You are also Goddess Mahalakshmi Herself. Worshipping and meditating upon Your sacred feet will bring one to the final state of liberation.

Kanakalasat kala sindhujalai ranuṣiñcati te guṇa raṅga bhuvam
bhajati sa kim na śacīkucakumbha taṭīparirambha sukhānu bhavam
tava caraṇam śaraṇam karavāṇi mṛḍāni sadāmayi dehi śivam
jaya jaya he mahiṣāsura-mardini ramyakapardini śailasute /19

O Mother! Even a simple sweeper in Your courtyard inherits all heavenly pleasures. Be pleased to accept my humble service and grant to me whatever You consider to be good for me.

Tava vimalendu kulam vadanendu malam sakalam nanukūlayate
kimu puruhūta purīndu mukhī sumukhī bhirasau vimukhī kriyate
mama tu matam śivanāmadhane bhavatī kṛpayā kimuta kriyate
jaya jaya he mahiṣāsura-mardini ramyakapardini śailasute /20

O Mother! None of the celestial beauties can even tempt one who meditates upon Your beautiful face. O Mother of Shiva's heart, do fulfill my life.

Ayi mayi dīnadayālutayā kṛpayaiva tvayā bhavitavyamume
ayi jagato jananī kṛpayāsi yathāsi tathānimitāsi rame
yaducita matra bhavatyurarī kurutāduru tāpamapākuru me
jaya jaya he mahiṣāsura-mardini ramyakapardini śailasute /21

O Mother! Uma! Are You not renowned for Your compassion? Be merciful to me, my Mother! Please grant to me the removal of all of my sorrows!

Śrī Lalitā Sahasranāma Stotram

The Thousand Names of the Divine Mother in Verse Form

Dhyānam

Sindūrāruṇa vigrahām tri nayanām māṇikya mauli sphurat
tārānāyaka śekharām smita mukhīm āpīna vakṣoruhām
pāṇibhyām alipūrṇa ratna caṣakam raktotpalam bibhratīm
saumyām ratna ghaṭastha rakta caraṇām dhyāyet parām ambikām

Dhyāyet padmāsanasthām vikasita vadanām padma patrāyatākṣīm
hemābhām pītavastrām kara kalita lasad hema padmām varāṅgīm
sarvālaṅkāra yuktām satatam abhayadām bhaktanamrām bhavānīm
śrīvidyām śāntamūrtīm sakala sura nutām sarva sampat pradātrīm

Sakuṅkuma vilepanām alika cumbi kastūrikām
samanda hasitekṣaṇām saśara cāpa pāśāṅkuśām
aśeṣa jana mohinīm aruṇa mālya bhūṣojvalām
japā kusuma bhāsurām japavidhau smaredambikām

Aruṇām karuṇā taraṅgitākṣīm dhṛta pāśāṅkuśa puṣpa bāṇa cāpām
aṇimādibhir āvṛtām mayūkhai raham ityeva vibhāvaye maheśīm

Stotram

1 Śrī-mātā śrī-mahā-rājñī śrīmat-siṁhāsaneśvarī
cid-agni-kuṇḍa-sambhūtā deva-kārya-samudyatā
2 Udyad-bhānu-sahasrābhā catur-bāhu-samanvitā
rāga-svarūpa-pāśāḍhyā krodhā-kārāṅkuś-ojjvalā
3 Mano-rūpekṣu-kodaṇḍā pañca-tanmātra-sāyakā
nijāruṇa-prabhāpūra-majjad-brahmāṇḍa-maṇḍalā
4 Campakāśoka-punnāga-saugandhika-lasat-kacā
kuruvinda-maṇi-śreṇī-kanat-koṭīra-maṇḍitā
5 Aṣṭamī-candra-vibhrāja-dalika-sthala-śobhitā
mukha-candra-kalaṅkābha-mṛganābhi-viśeṣakā

6 Vadana-smara-māṅgalya-gṛha-toraṇa-cillikā
vaktra-lakṣmī-parīvāha-calan-mīnābha-locanā
7 Nava-campaka-puṣpābha-nāsā-daṇḍa-virājitā
tārā-kānti-tiraskāri-nāsābharaṇa-bhāsurā
8 Kadamba-mañjarī-kḷpta-karṇa-pūra-manoharā
tāṭaṅka-yugalī-bhūta-tapanoḍupa-maṇḍalā
9 Padma-rāga-śilādarśa-paribhāvi-kapola-bhūḥ
nava-vidruma-bimba-śrī-nyakkāri-radana-cchadā
10 Śuddha-vidyāṅkurākāra-dvija-paṅkti-dvayojjvalā
karpūra-vīṭikāmoda-samākarṣad-digantarā
11 Nija-sallāpa-mādhurya-vinirbhartsita-kacchapī
manda-smita-prabhā-pūra-majjat-kāmeśa-mānasā
12 Anākalita-sādṛśya-cibuka-śrī-virājitā
kāmeśa-baddha-māṅgalya-sūtra-śobhita-kandharā

13 Kanakāṅgada-keyūra-kamanīya-bhujānvitā
ratna-graiveya-cintāka-lola-muktā-phalānvitā

14 Kāmeśvara-prema-ratna-maṇi-pratipaṇa-stanī
nābhyāla-vāla-romāli-latā-phala-kuca-dvayī

15 Lakṣya-roma-latā-dhāratā-sumunneya-madhyamā
stana-bhāra-dalan-madhya-paṭṭa-bandha-vali-trayā

16 Aruṇāruṇa-kausumbha-vastra-bhāsvat-kaṭī-taṭī
ratna-kinkiṇikā-ramya-raśanā-dāma-bhūṣitā

17 Kāmeśa-jñāta-saubhāgya-mārdavoru-dvayānvitā
māṇikya-mukuṭākāra-jānu-dvaya-virājitā

18 Indra-gopa-parikṣipta-smara-tūṇābha-jaṅghikā
gūḍha-gulphā kūrma-pṛṣṭha-jayiṣṇu-prapadānvitā

19 Nakha-dīdhiti-sañchanna-namajjana-tamoguṇa
pada-dvaya-prabhā-jāla-parākṛta-saroruhā

20 Śiñjāna-maṇi-mañjīra-maṇḍita-śrī-padāmbujā
marālī-manda-gamanā mahā-lāvaṇya-śevadhiḥ

21 Sarvāruṇā'navadyāṅgī sarvābharaṇa-bhūṣitā
śiva-kāmeśvarāṅkasthā śivā svādhīna-vallabhā

22 Sumeru-madhya-śṛṅgasthā śrīman-nagara-nāyikā
cintāmaṇi-gṛhāntasthā pañca-brahmāsana-sthitā

23 Mahā-padmāṭavī-saṁsthā kadamba-vana-vāsinī
sudhā-sāgara-madhyasthā kāmākṣī kāmadāyinī

24 Devarṣi-gaṇa-saṅghāta-stūyamānātma-vaibhavā
bhaṇḍāsura-vadhodyukta-śakti-senā-samanvitā

25 Sampatkarī-samārūḍha-sindhura-vraja-sevitā
aśvārūḍhādhiṣṭhitāśva-koṭi-koṭibhir-āvṛtā

26 Cakra-rāja-rathārūḍha-sarvāyudha-pariṣkṛtā
geya-cakra-rathārūḍha-mantriṇī-parisevitā

27 Kiricakra-rathārūḍha-daṇḍanāthā-puras-kṛtā
jvālā-mālinikākṣipta-vahni-prākāra-madhyagā

28 Bhaṇḍa-sainya-vadhodyukta-śakti-vikrama-harṣitā
nityā-parākramāṭopa-nirīkṣaṇa-samutsukā

29 Bhaṇḍa-putra-vadhodyukta-bālā-vikrama-nanditā
mantriṇyambā-viracita-viṣaṅga-vadha-toṣitā

30 Viśukra-prāṇa-haraṇa-vārāhī-vīrya-nanditā
kāmeśvara-mukhāloka-kalpita-śrī-gaṇeśvarā

31 Mahā-gaṇeśa-nirbhinna-vighna-yantra-praharṣitā
bhaṇḍāsurendra-nirmukta-śastra-pratyastra-varṣiṇī

32 Karāṅguli-nakhotpanna-nārāyaṇa-daśākṛtiḥ
mahā-pāśupatāstrāgni-nirdagdhāsura-sainikā

33 Kāmeśvarāstra-nirdagdha-sabhaṇḍāsura-śūnyakā
brahmopendra-mahendrādi-deva-saṁstuta-vaibhavā

34 Hara-netrāgni-sandagdha-kāma-sañjīvanauṣadhiḥ
śrīmad-vāgbhava-kūṭaika-svarūpa-mukha-paṅkajā

35 Kaṇṭhādhaḥ-kaṭi-paryanta-madhya-kūṭa-svarūpiṇī
śakti-kūṭaikatāpanna-kaṭyadhobhāga-dhāriṇī

36 Mūla-mantrātmikā mūla-kūṭa-traya-kalebarā
kulāmṛtaika-rasikā kula-saṅketa-pālinī

37 Kulāṅganā kulāntasthā kaulinī kula-yoginī
akulā samayāntasthā samayācāra-tatparā

38 Mūlādhāraika-nilayā brahma-granthi-vibhedinī
maṇipūrāntar-uditā viṣṇu-granthi-vibhedinī

39 Ājñā-cakrāntarālasthā rudra-granthi-vibhedinī
sahasrārāmbujārūḍhā sudhā-sārābhi-varṣiṇī

40 Taḍil-latā-sama-ruciḥ ṣaṭ-cakropari-saṁsthitā
mahā-saktiḥ kuṇḍalinī bisa-tantu-tanīyasī

41 Bhavānī bhāvanāgamyā bhavāraṇya-kuṭhārikā
bhadra-priyā bhadra-mūrtir bhakta-saubhāgya-dāyinī

42 Bhakti-priyā bhakti-gamyā bhakti-vaśyā bhayāpahā
śāmbhavī śāradārādhyā śarvāṇī śarma-dāyinī

43 Śāṅkarī śrīkarī sādhvī śarac-candra-nibhānanā
śātodarī śāntimatī nirādhārā nirañjanā

44 Nirlepā nirmalā nityā nirākārā nirākulā
nirguṇā niṣkalā śāntā niṣkāmā nirupaplavā

45 Nitya-muktā nirvikārā niṣprapañcā nirāśrayā
nitya-śuddhā nitya-buddhā niravadyā nirantarā

46 Niṣkāraṇā niṣkalaṅkā nirupādhir nirīśvarā
nīrāgā rāga-mathanā nirmadā mada-nāśinī

47 Niścintā nirahaṅkārā nirmohā moha-nāśinī
nirmamā mamatā-hantrī niṣpāpā pāpa-nāśinī

48 Niṣkrodhā krodha-śamanī nirlobhā lobha-nāśinī
niḥsaṁśayā saṁśaya-ghnī nirbhavā bhava-nāśinī

49 Nirvikalpā nirābādhā nirbhedā bheda-nāśinī
nirnāśā mṛtyu-mathanī niṣkriyā niṣparigrahā

50 Nistulā nīla-cikurā nirapāyā niratyayā
durlabhā durgamā durgā duḥkha-hantrī sukha-pradā

51 Duṣṭadūrā durācāra-śamanī doṣa-varjitā
sarvajñā sāndrakaruṇā samānādhika-varjitā

52 Sarva-śakti-mayī sarva-maṅgalā sad-gati-pradā
sarveśvarī sarva-mayī sarva-mantra-svarūpiṇī

53 Sarva-yantrātmikā sarva-tantra-rūpā manonmanī
māheśvarī mahā-devī mahā-lakṣmī mṛḍa-priyā

54 Mahā-rūpā mahā-pūjyā mahā-pātaka-nāśinī
mahā-māyā mahā-sattvā mahā-śaktir mahā-ratiḥ

55 Mahā-bhogā mahaiśvaryā mahā-vīryā mahā-balā
mahā-buddhir mahā-siddhir mahā-yogeśvareśvarī

56 Mahā-tantrā mahā-mantrā mahā-yantrā mahāsanā
mahā-yāga-kramārādhyā mahā-bhairava-pūjitā

57 Maheśvara-mahākalpa-mahātāṇḍava-sākṣiṇī
mahā-kāmeśa-mahiṣī mahā-tripura-sundarī

58 Catuḥ-ṣaṣtyupacārāḍhyā catuḥ-ṣaṣṭi-kalāmayī
mahā-catuḥ-ṣaṣṭi-koṭi-yoginī-gaṇa-sevitā

59 Manu-vidyā candra-vidyā candra-maṇḍala-madhyagā
cāru-rūpā cāru-hāsā cāru-candra-kalā-dharā

60 Carācara-jagan-nāthā cakra-rāja-niketanā
pārvatī padma-nayanā padma-rāga-sama-prabhā

61 Pañca-pretāsanāsīnā pañca-brahma-svarūpiṇī
cinmayī paramānandā vijñāna-ghana-rūpiṇī

62 Dhyāna-dhyātṛ-dhyeya-rūpā dharmādharma-vivarjitā
viśva-rūpā jāgariṇī svapantī taijasātmikā

63 Suptā prājñātmikā turyā sarvāvasthā-vivarjitā
sṛṣṭi-kartrī brahma-rūpā goptrī govinda-rūpiṇī

64 Saṁhāriṇī rudra-rūpā tirodhāna-kar'īśvarī
sadā-śivā'nugraha-dā pañca-kṛtya-parāyaṇā

65 Bhānu-maṇḍala-madhyasthā bhairavī bhaga-mālinī
padmāsanā bhagavatī padma-nābha-sahodarī

66 Unmeṣa-nimiṣotpanna-vipanna-bhuvanāvalī
sahasra-śīrṣa-vadanā sahasrākṣī sahasra-pāt

67 Ābrahma-kīṭa-jananī varṇāśrama-vidhāyinī
nijājñā-rūpa-nigamā puṇyāpuṇya-phala-pradā

68 Śruti-sīmanta-sindūrī-kṛta-pādābja-dhūlikā
sakalāgama-sandoha-śukti-sampuṭa-mauktikā

69 Puruṣārtha-pradā pūrṇā bhoginī bhuvaneśvarī
ambikā'nādi-nidhanā hari-brahmendra-sevitā

70 Nārāyaṇī nāda-rūpā nāma-rūpa-vivarjitā
hrīṅ-kārī hrīmatī hṛdyā heyopādeya-varjitā

71 Rāja-rājārcitā rājñī ramyā rājīva-locanā
rañjanī ramaṇī rasyā raṇat-kiṅkiṇi-mekhalā

72 Ramā rākendu-vadanā rati-rūpā rati-priyā
rakṣā-karī rākṣasa-ghnī rāmā ramaṇa-lampaṭā

73 Kāmyā kāma-kalā-rūpā kadamba-kusuma-priyā
kalyāṇī jagatī-kandā karuṇā-rasa-sāgarā

74 Kalāvatī kalālāpā kāntā kādambarī-priyā
varadā vāma-nayanā vāruṇī-mada-vihvalā

75 Viśvādhikā vedavedyā vindhyācala-nivāsinī
vidhātrī veda-jananī viṣṇu-māyā vilāsinī

76 Kṣetra-svarūpā kṣetreśī kṣetra-kṣetrajña-pālinī
kṣaya-vṛddhi-vinirmuktā kṣetra-pāla-samarcitā

77 Vijayā vimalā vandyā vandāru-jana-vatsalā
vāg-vādinī vāma-keśī vahni-maṇḍala-vāsinī

78 Bhaktimat-kalpa-latikā paśu-pāśa-vimocinī
saṁhṛtāśeṣa-pāṣaṇḍā sadācāra-pravartikā

79 Tāpa-trayāgni-santapta-samāhlādana-candrikā
taruṇī tāpasārādhyā tanu-madhyā tamopahā
80 Citis tat-pada-lakṣyārthā cid-eka-rasa-rūpiṇī
svātmānanda-lavī-bhūta-brahmādyānanda-santatiḥ
81 Parā pratyak-citī-rūpā paśyantī para-devatā
madhyamā vaikharī-rūpā bhakta-mānasa-haṁsikā
82 Kāmeśvara-prāṇa-nāḍī kṛtajñā kāma-pūjitā
śṛṅgāra-rasa-sampūrṇā jayā jālandhara-sthitā
83 Oḍyāṇa-pīṭha-nilayā bindu-maṇḍala-vāsinī
raho-yāga-kramārādhyā rahas-tarpaṇa-tarpitā
84 Sadyaḥ-prasādinī viśva-sākṣiṇī sākṣi-varjitā
ṣaḍ-aṅga-devatā-yuktā ṣāḍ-guṇya-paripūritā

85 Nitya-klinnā nirupamā nirvāṇa-sukha-dāyinī
nityā-ṣoḍaśikā-rūpā śrīkaṇṭhārdha-śarīriṇī

86 Prabhāvatī prabhā-rūpā prasiddhā parameśvarī
mūla-prakṛtir avyaktā vyaktāvyakta-svarūpiṇī

87 Vyāpinī vividhākārā vidyāvidyā-svarūpiṇī
mahā-kāmeśa-nayana-kumudāhlāda-kaumudī

88 Bhakta-hārda-tamo-bheda-bhānumad-bhānu-santatīḥ
śiva-dūtī śivārādhyā śiva-mūrtiḥ śivaṅkarī

89 Śiva-priyā śiva-parā śiṣṭeṣṭā śiṣṭapūjitā
aprameyā svaprakāśā mano-vācām-agocarā

90 Cicchaktiś cetanā-rūpā jaḍa-śaktir jaḍātmikā
gāyatrī vyāhṛtiḥ sandyā dvija-vṛnda-niṣevitā

91 Tattvāsanā tat'vam'ayī pañca-kośāntara-sthitā
niḥsīma-mahimā nitya-yauvanā mada-śālinī
92 Mada-ghūrṇita-raktākṣī mada-pāṭala-gaṇḍa-bhūḥ
candana-drava-digdhāṅgī cāmpeya-kusuma-priyā
93 Kuśalā komalākārā kurukullā kuleśvarī
kula-kuṇḍālayā kaula-mārga-tatpara-sevitā
94 Kumāra-gaṇanāthāmbā tuṣṭiḥ puṣṭir matir dhṛtiḥ
śāntiḥ svasti-matī kāntir nandinī vighna-nāśinī
95 Tejovatī tri-nayanā lolākṣī-kāma-rūpiṇī
mālinī haṁsinī mātā malayācala-vāsinī
96 Sumukhī nalinī subhrūḥ śobhanā suranāyikā
kālakaṇṭhī kānti-matī kṣobhiṇī sūkṣma-rūpiṇī

97 Vajreśvarī vāma-devī vayovasthā-vivarjitā
siddheśvarī siddha-vidyā siddha-mātā yaśasvinī

98 Viśuddhi-cakra-nilayā'rakta-varṇā tri-locanā
khaṭvāṅgādi-praharaṇā vadanaika-samanvitā

99 Pāyasānna-priyā tvaksthā paśu-loka-bhayaṅkarī
amṛtādi-mahāśakti-saṁvṛtā ḍākinīśvarī

100 Anāhatābja-nilayā śyāmābhā vadana-dvayā
daṁṣṭrojjvalā'kṣa-mālādi-dharā rudhira-saṁsthitā

101 Kāla-rātryādi-śaktyaugha-vṛtā snigdhaudana-priyā
mahā-vīrendra-varadā rākiṇyambā-svarūpiṇī

102 Maṇipūrābja-nilayā vadana-traya-samyutā
vajrādikāyudhopetā ḍāmaryādibhir-āvṛtā

103 Rakta-varṇā māṁsa-niṣṭhā guḍānna-prīta-mānasā
samasta-bhakta-sukhadā lākinyambā-svarūpiṇī

104 Svādhiṣṭhānāmbuja-gatā catur-vaktra-manoharā
śūlādyāyudha-sampannā pīta-varṇā'ti-garvitā

105 Medo-niṣṭhā madhu-prītā bandhinyādi-samanvitā
dadhyannāsakta-hṛdayā kākinī-rūpa-dhāriṇī

106 Mūlādhārāmbujārūḍhā pañca-vaktrā'sthi-saṁsthitā
aṅkuśādi-praharaṇā varadādi-niṣevitā

107 Mudgaudanāsakta-cittā sākinyambā-svarūpiṇī
ājñā-cakrābja-nilayā śukla-varṇā ṣad-ānanā

108 Majjā-saṁsthā haṁsavatī-mukhya-śakti-samanvitā
haridrānnaika-rasikā hākinī-rūpa-dhāriṇī

109 Sahasra-dala-padmasthā sarva-varṇopaśobhitā
sarvāyudha-dharā śukla-saṁsthitā sarvatomukhī

110 Sarvaudana-prīta-cittā yākinyambā-svarūpiṇī
svāhā svadhā'matir medhā śruti smṛtir anuttamā

111 Puṇya-kīrtiḥ puṇya-labhyā puṇya-śravaṇa-kīrtanā
pulomajārcitā bandha-mocanī barbarālakā

112 Vimarśa-rūpiṇī vidyā viyadādi-jagat-prasūḥ
sarva-vyādhi-praśamanī sarva-mṛtyu-nivāriṇī

113 Agra-gaṇyā'cintya-rūpā kali-kalmaṣa-nāśinī
kātyāyanī kālahantrī kamalākṣa-niṣevitā

114 Tāmbūla-pūrita-mukhī dāḍimī-kusuma-prabhā
mṛgākṣī mohinī mukhyā mṛḍānī mitra-rūpiṇī

115 Nitya-tṛptā bhakta-nidhir niyantrī nikhileśvarī
maitryādi-vāsanā-labhyā mahā-pralaya-sākṣiṇī

116 Parāśaktiḥ parāniṣṭhā prajñāna-ghana-rūpiṇī
mādhvī-pānālasā mattā mātṛkā-varṇa-rūpiṇī

117 Mahākailāsa-nilayā mṛṇāla-mṛdu-dor-latā
mahanīyā dayā-mūrtir mahā-sāmrājya-śālinī

118 Ātma-vidyā mahā-vidyā śrī-vidyā kāma-sevitā
śrī-ṣoḍaśākṣarī-vidyā trikūṭā kāma-koṭikā

119 Kaṭākṣa-kiṅkarī-bhūta-kamalā-koṭi-sevitā
śiraḥsthitā candra-nibhā bhālasth'endra-dhanuḥ-prabhā

120 Hṛdayasthā ravi-prakhyā trikoṇāntara-dīpikā
dākṣāyaṇī daitya-hantrī dakṣa-yajña-vināśinī

121 Darāndolita-dīrghākṣī dara-hāsojjvalan-mukhī
guru-mūrtir guṇa-nidhir go-mātā guha-janma-bhūḥ

122 Deveśī daṇḍa-nītisthā daharākāśa-rūpiṇī
pratipan-mukhya-rākānta-tithi-maṇḍala-pūjitā

123 Kalātmikā kalā-nāthā kāvyālāpa-vinodinī
sacāmara-ramā-vāṇī-savya-dakṣiṇa-sevitā

124 Ādiśaktir ameyā'tmā paramā pāvanākṛtiḥ
aneka-koṭi-brahmāṇḍa-jananī divya-vigrahā

125 Klīṅkārī kevalā guhyā kaivalya-pada-dāyinī
tripurā trijagad-vandyā trimūrtir tridaśeśvarī

126 Tryakṣarī divya-gandhāḍhyā sindūra-tilakāñcitā
umā śailendra-tanayā gaurī gandharva-sevitā

127 Viśva-garbhā svarṇa-garbhā'varadā vāg-adhīśvarī
dhyāna-gamyā'pari-cchedyā jñānadā jñāna-vigrahā
128 Sarva-vedānta-saṁvedyā satyānanda-svarūpiṇī
lopāmudrārcitā līlā-klṛpta-brahmāṇḍa-maṇḍalā
129 Adṛśyā dṛśya-rahitā vijñātrī vedya-varjitā
yoginī yogadā yogyā yogānandā yugandharā
130 Icchā-śakti-jñāna-śakti-kriyā-śakti-svarūpiṇī
sarvādhārā supratiṣṭhā sad-asad-rūpa-dhāriṇī
131 Aṣṭa-mūrtir ajā-jaitrī loka-yātrā-vidhāyinī
ekākinī bhūma-rūpā nirdvaitā dvaita-varjitā
132 Annadā vasudā vṛddhā brahmātmaikya-svarūpiṇī
bṛhatī brāhmaṇī brāhmī brahmānandā bali-priyā

133 Bhāṣā-rūpā bṛhat-senā bhāvābhāva-vivarjitā
sukhārādhyā śubha-karī śobhanā-sulabhā-gatiḥ

134 Rāja-rājeśvarī rājya-dāyinī rājya-vallabhā
rājat-kṛpā rāja-pīṭha-niveśita-nijāśritā

135 Rājya-lakṣmīḥ kośa-nāthā catur-aṅga-baleśvarī
sāmrājya-dāyinī satya-sandhā sāgara-mekhalā

136 Dīkṣitā daitya-śamanī sarva-loka-vaśaṅkarī
sarvārtha-dātrī sāvitrī sac-cid-ānanda-rūpiṇī

137 Deśa-kālāparicchinnā sarvagā sarva-mohinī
sarasvatī śāstramayī guhāmbā guhya-rūpiṇī

138 Sarvopādhi-vinirmuktā sadāśiva-pativratā
sampradāyeśvarī sādhv'ī guru-maṇḍala-rūpiṇī

139 Kulottīrṇā bhagārādhyā māyā madhumatī mahī
gaṇāmbā guhyakārādhyā komalāṅgī guru-priyā

140 Svatantrā sarva-tantreśī dakṣiṇā-mūrti-rūpiṇī
sanakādi-samārādhyā śiva-jñāna-pradāyinī

141 Cit-kalā'nanda-kalikā prema-rūpā priyaṅkarī
nāma-pārāyaṇa-prītā nandi-vidyā naṭeśvarī

142 Mithyā-jagad-adhiṣṭhānā muktidā mukti-rūpiṇī
lāsya-priyā laya-karī lajjā rambhādi-vanditā

143 Bhava-dāva-sudhā-vṛṣṭiḥ pāpāraṇya-davānalā
daurbhāgya-tūla-vātūlā jarā-dhvānta-ravi-prabhā

144 Bhāgyābdhi-candrikā bhakta-citta-keki-ghanāghanā
roga-parvata-dambholir mṛtyu-dāru-kuṭhārikā

145 Maheśvarī mahā-kālī mahā-grāsā mahāśanā
aparṇā caṇḍikā caṇḍa-muṇḍāsura-niṣūdinī

146 Kṣarākṣarātmikā sarva-lokeśī viśva-dhāriṇī
tri-varga-dātrī subhagā tryambakā triguṇātmikā

147 Svargāpavargadā śuddhā japā-puṣpa-nibhākṛtiḥ
ojovatī dyuti-dharā yajña-rūpā priya-vratā

148 Durārādhyā durādharṣā pāṭalī-kusuma-priyā
mahatī meru-nilayā mandāra-kusuma-priyā

149 Vīrārādhyā virāḍ-rūpā virajā viśvato-mukhī
pratyag-rūpā parākāśā prāṇadā prāṇa-rūpiṇī

150 Mārtāṇḍa-bhairavārādhyā mantriṇī-nyasta-rājya-dhūḥ
tripureśī jayat-senā nistraiguṇyā parāparā

151 Satya-jñānānanda-rūpā sāmarasya-parāyaṇā
kapardinī kalā-mālā kāma-dhuk kāma-rūpiṇī
152 Kalā-nidhiḥ kāvya-kalā rasa-jñā rasa-śevadhiḥ
puṣṭā purātanā pūjyā puṣkarā puṣkarekṣaṇā
153 Param-jyotiḥ param-dhāma paramāṇuḥ parāt-parā
pāśa-hastā pāśa-hantrī para-mantra-vibhedinī
154 Mūrtā'mūrtā'nitya-tṛptā muni-mānasa-haṁsikā
satya-vratā satya-rūpā sarvāntar-yāminī satī
155 Brahmāṇī brahma jananī bahu-rūpā budhārcitā
prasavitrī pracaṇḍā'jñā pratiṣṭhā prakaṭākṛtiḥ
156 Prāṇeśvarī prāṇa-dātrī pañcāśat-pīṭha-rūpiṇī
viśṛṅkhalā viviktasthā vīra-mātā viyat-prasūḥ

157 Mukundā mukti-nilayā mūla-vigraha-rūpiṇī
bhāva-jñā bhava-roga-ghnī bhava-cakra-pravartinī

158 Chandaḥ-sārā śāstra-sārā mantra-sārā talodarī
udāra-kīrtir uddāma-vaibhavā varṇa-rūpiṇī

159 Janma-mṛtyu-jarā-tapta-jana-viśrānti-dāyinī
sarvopaniṣad-udghuṣṭā śāntyatīta-kalātmikā

160 Gambhīrā gaganāntaḥsthā garvitā gāna-lolupā
kalpanā-rahitā kāṣṭhā'kāntā kāntārdha-vigrahā

161 Kārya-kāraṇa-nirmuktā kāma-keli-taraṅgitā
kanat-kanaka-tāṭaṅkā līlā-vigraha-dhāriṇī

162 Ajā kṣaya-vinirmuktā mugdhā kṣipra-prasādinī
antar-mukha-samārādhyā bahir-mukha-sudurlabhā

163 Trayī trivarga-nilayā tristhā tripura-mālinī
nir-āmayā nir-ālambā svātmārāmā sudhāsṛtiḥ
164 Saṁsāra-paṅka-nirmagna-samuddharaṇa-paṇḍitā
yajña-priyā yajña-kartrī yajamāna-svarūpiṇī
165 Dharmādhārā dhanādhyakṣā dhana-dhānya-vivardhinī
vipra-priyā vipra-rūpā viśva-bhramaṇa-kāriṇī
166 Viśva-grāsā vidrumābhā vaiṣṇavī viṣṇu-rūpiṇī
ayonir yoni-nilayā kūṭasthā kula-rūpiṇī
167 Vīra-goṣṭhī-priyā vīrā naiṣkarmyā nāda-rūpiṇī
vijñāna-kalanā kalyā vidagdhā baindavāsanā
168 Tattvādhikā tattva-mayī tat-tvam-artha-svarūpiṇī
sāma-gāna-priyā somyā sadāśiva-kuṭumbinī

169 Savyāpasavya-mārgasthā sarvāpad-vinivāriṇī
svasthā svabhāva-madhurā dhīrā dhīra-samarcitā

170 Caitanyārghya-samārādhyā caitanya-kusuma-priyā
sadoditā sadā-tuṣṭā taruṇāditya-pāṭalā

171 Dakṣiṇādakṣiṇārādhyā dara-smera-mukhāmbujā
kaulinī-kevalā'narghya-kaivalya-pada-dāyinī

172 Stotra-priyā stuti-matī śruti-saṁstuta-vaibhavā
manasvinī mānavatī maheśī maṅgalākṛtiḥ

173 Viśva-mātā jagad-dhātrī viśālākṣī virāgiṇī
pragalbhā paramodārā parā-modā manomayī

174 Vyoma-keśī vimānasthā vajriṇī vāmakeśvarī
pañca-yajña-priyā pañca-preta-mañcādhi-śāyinī

175 Pañcamī pañca-bhūteśī pañca-saṅkhyopacāriṇī
śāśvatī śāśvataiśvaryā śarmadā śambhu-mohinī

176 Dharā dhara-sutā dhanyā dharmiṇī dharma-vardhinī
lokātītā guṇātītā sarvātītā śamātmikā

177 Bandhūka-kusuma-prakhyā bālā līlā-vinodinī
sumaṅgalī sukha-karī suveṣāḍhyā suvāsinī

178 Suvāsinyarcana-prītā'śobhanā śuddha-mānasā
bindu-tarpaṇa-santuṣṭā pūrvajā tripurāmbikā

179 Daśa-mudrā-samārādhyā tripurāśrī-vaśaṅkarī
jñāna-mudrā jñāna-gamyā jñāna-jñeya-svarūpiṇī

180 Yoni-mudrā trikhaṇḍeśī triguṇā'mbā trikoṇagā
anaghā'dbhuta-cāritrā vāñchitārtha-pradāyinī

181 Abhyāsātiśaya-jñātā ṣaḍadhvātīta-rūpiṇī
avyāja-karuṇā-mūrtir ajñāna-dhvānta-dīpikā

182 Ābāla-gopa-viditā sarvānullaṅghya-śāsanā
śrīcakra-rāja-nilayā śrīmat-tripura-sundarī

183 Śrī-śivā śiva-śaktyaikya-rūpiṇī lalitāmbikā

Śrī Lalitā Triśatī Stotra

1. Om kakāra rūpāyai namaḥ

She who is the letter 'ka'. (This letter represents light. It is the first letter of the 'pañcadasākṣari' mantra, the 15 syllable mantra).

2. Om kalyāṇyai namaḥ

She who is auspicious.

3. Om kalyāṇa guṇa śāliṇyai namaḥ

She who is the personification of good qualities.

4. Om kalyāṇa śaila nilayāyai namaḥ

She who resides in the auspicious mountain (Himalaya).

5. Om kamanīyāyai namaḥ

She who is desirable.

6. Om kalāvatyai namaḥ

She who possesses all arts.

7. Om kamalākṣyai namaḥ
She who has lotus-like eyes.

8. Om kanmaṣa ghnyai namaḥ
She who destroys impurities.

9. Om karuṇāmṛta sāgarāyai namaḥ
She who is the Ocean of the nectar of compassion.

10. Om kadamba kānanā vāsāyai namaḥ
She who lives in the forest of Kadamba trees (a blue flowering tree).

11. Om kadamba kusuma priyāyai namaḥ
She who likes the flowers of the Kadamba tree.

12. Om kandarpa vidyāyai namaḥ
She who is the knowledge used by Cupid.

13. Om kandarpa janakāpāṅga vīkṣaṇāyai namaḥ
She who created Cupid by her glance alone.

14. Om karpūra vīṭi saurabhya kallolita kakuptaṭāyai namaḥ

She whose mouth is fragrant from chewing on the betel leaf, mixed with camphor and other ingredients.

15. Om kali doṣa harāyai namaḥ

She who destroys the bad effects of Kali yuga.

16. Om kañja locanāyai namaḥ

She who has eyes like a lotus.

17. Om kamra vigrahāyai namaḥ

She who has a desirable form.

18. Om karmādi sākṣiṇyai namaḥ

She who is the witness of actions, thought and words.

19. Om kārayitryaī namaḥ

She who controls all actions.

20. Om karma phala pradāyai namaḥ

She who gives the fruit of one's actions.

21. Om ekāra rūpāyai namaḥ

She who is the letter 'e'. ('E' denotes the absolute truth, Brahman. It is the second letter of the 'pañcadasākṣari' mantra.)

22. Om ekākṣaryai namaḥ

She who is the single syllable ('Om').

23. Om ekānekākṣarā kṛtāyai namaḥ

She who manifests the single syllable 'Om', and all other letters as well.

24. Om etat tadityanirdeśyāyai namaḥ

She who cannot be indicated as 'this' or 'that'.

25. Om ekānanda cidākṛtayai namaḥ

She who is the form of non-dual bliss and consciousness.

26. Om evam ityāgamābodhyāyai namaḥ

She whom the Vedas cannot describe.

27. Om eka bhaktimad arcitāyai namaḥ

She who is worshipped by those with one-pointed devotion.

28. Om ekāgra citta nirdhyātāyai namaḥ
She who can be meditated on by a one-pointed mind.

29. Om eṣaṇā rahitā dṛtāyai namaḥ
She who is the refuge of those without worldly desires.

30. Om elā sugandhi cikurāyai namaḥ
She whose hair has the sweet smell of cardamom.

31. Om enaḥ kūṭa vināśinyai namaḥ
She who destroys bundles of impurities.

32. Om eka bhogāyai namaḥ
She who has only one experience (Self-experience).

33. Om eka rasāyai namaḥ
She who has only Bliss (Bliss of the Self).

34. Om ekaiśvarya pradāyinyai namaḥ
She who gives the glory of Oneness.

35. Om ekātapatra sāmrājya pradāyai namaḥ
She who gives you the power of the emperor of the world.

36. Om ekānta pūjitāyai namaḥ
She who is worshipped with a one-pointed mind.

37. Om edhamāna prabhāyai namaḥ
She who has the foremost luster.

38. Om ekad aneka jagadīśvaryai namaḥ
She who is the Ruler of the universe of Oneness and duality.

39. Om eka vīrādi samsevyāyai namaḥ
She who is worshipped by valorous warriors.

40. Om eka prābhava śālinyai namaḥ
She who has the power of the One Truth.

41. Om īkāra rūpāyai namaḥ
She who is the letter 'ī'. ('Ī' denotes Shakti. It is the third letter of the 'pañcadasākṣari' mantra.)

42. Om īśitryai namaḥ

She who rules everything.

43. Om īpsitārtha pradāyinyai namaḥ

She who gives the objects one desires.

44. Om īdṛgityavinird eśyāyai namaḥ

She who cannot be indicated by attributes.

45. Om īśvaratva vidhāyinyai namaḥ

She who makes Brahman into the Creator, Sustainer and Destroyer.

46. Om īśānādi brahma mayyai namaḥ

She who is in the form of the five gods, Brahma, Vishnu, Rudra, Īsha, and Sadāshiva.

47. Om īśitvādyaṣṭa siddhidāyai namaḥ

She who gives the eight super-natural powers.

48. Om īkṣitryai namaḥ

She who sees all.

49. Om īkṣaṇa sṛṣṭāṇḍa koṭyai namaḥ
She who creates millions of galaxies by a mere glance.

50. Om īśvara vallabhāyai namaḥ
She who is the beloved of Shiva.

51. Om īḍitāyai namaḥ
She who is praised in the holy books like Vedas, Puranas, etc.

52. Om īśvarārdhāṅga śarīrāyai namaḥ
She whose body is half Shiva.

53. Om īśādhi devatāyai namaḥ
She who is deity supreme even to Shiva.

54. Om īśvara preraṇa karyai namaḥ
She who prompts the actions of Shiva (Creation, etc.).

55. Om īśa tāṇḍava sākṣiṇyai namaḥ
She who is the witness of the cosmic dance of Shiva.

56. Om īśvarotsaṅga nilayāyai namaḥ

She who abides in union with Shiva.

57. Om īti bādhā vināśinyai namaḥ

She who destroys unexpected calamities.

58. Om īhā virahitāyai namaḥ

She who is devoid of desire.

59. Om īśa śaktyai namaḥ

She who is the power of Shiva.

60. Om īṣat smitānanāyai namaḥ

She who has a soft smile on Her face.

61. Om lakāra rūpāyai namaḥ

She who is the letter 'la'. ('La' denotes the wave which initiates wisdom. It is the fourth letter of the 'pañcadasākṣari' mantra.)

62. Om lalitāyai namaḥ

She who is known by the name of 'Lalitā'.

63. Om lakṣmī vāṇī niṣevitāyai namaḥ

She who is attended on by Lakshmi (the goddess of wealth) and Saraswati (the goddess of knowledge).

64. Om lākinyai namaḥ

She who is easily approachable.

65. Om lalanā rūpāyai namaḥ

She who can be seen as the goddess in all women.

66. Om lasad dāḍima pāṭalāyai namaḥ

She whose skin is the color of a blossomed pomegranate flower.

67. Om lasantikā lasat phālāyai namaḥ

She who has a shining forehead with the beautiful *tilaka* (dot).

68. Om lalāṭa nayanārcitāyai namaḥ

She who is worshipped by yogis whose eyes of wisdom are awakened.

69. Om lakṣaṇojjvala divyāṅgyai namaḥ

She whose limbs have all auspicious qualities.

70. Om lakṣa koṭyaṇḍa nāyikāyai namaḥ

She who rules billions of galaxies.

71. Om lakṣyārthāyai namaḥ

She who is the inner experience behind all the Vedic proclamations.

72. Om lakṣaṇāgamyāyai namaḥ

She who cannot be understood by characteristics.

73. Om labdhakāmāyai namaḥ

She whose desires are fulfilled.

74. Om latātanave namah

She whose body resembles a fine creeper.

75. Om lalāmarā jadalikāyai namaḥ

She who has a *tilaka* made of musk on the forehead.

76. Om lambi muktā latāñcitāyai namaḥ

She who is decorated with a hanging pearl heelball.

77. Om lambodara prasave namaḥ
She who is the mother of Ganesha.

78. Om labhyāyai namaḥ
She who is attainable.

79. Om lajjāḍhyāyai namaḥ
She who has the quality of shyness.

80. Omlaya varjitāyai namaḥ
She who is never destroyed.

81. Om hrīmkāra rūpāyai namaḥ
She who is the sacred syllable 'hrīm'. (The fifth letter of the 'pañcadasākṣari' mantra.)

82. Om hrīmkāra nilayāyai namaḥ
She who abides in the sacred syllable 'hrīm'.

83. Om hrīm pada priyāyai namaḥ
She who is fond of the mantra 'hrīm'.

84. Om hrīmkāra bījāyai namaḥ

She who is the seed of the sound 'hrīm'.

85. Om hrīmkāra mantrāyai namaḥ

She whose mantra is the sound 'hrīm'.

86. Om hrīmkāra lakṣaṇāyai namaḥ

She who is indicated by the sound 'hrīm'.

87. Om hrīmkāra japa suprītāyai namaḥ

She who is very pleased by japa of 'hrīm'.

88. Om hrīmatyai namaḥ

She who is endowed with modesty.

89. Om hrīm vibhūṣaṇāyai namaḥ

She whose ornament is the sound 'hrīm'.

90. Om hrīm śīlāyai namaḥ

She who manifests 'hrīm'.

91. Om hrīm padārādhyāyai namaḥ
She who is worshipped by the sound 'hrīm'.

92. Om hrīm garbhāyai namaḥ
She who is the source of 'hrīm'.

93. Om hrīm padābidhāyai namaḥ
She who is known by the sound 'hrīm'.

94. Om hrīmkāra vācyāyai namaḥ
She who is indicated by 'hrīm'.

95. Om hrīmkāra pūjyāyai namaḥ
She who is to be worshipped by 'hrīm'.

96. Om hrīmkāra pīṭhikāyai namaḥ
She who is the basis of 'hrīm'.

97. Om hrīmkāra vedyāyai namaḥ
She who is known by 'hrīm'.

98. Om hrīmkāra cintyāyai namaḥ

She who can be thought of through 'hrīm'.

99. Om hrīm namaḥ

She who is 'hrīm'.

100. Om hrīm śarīriṇyai namaḥ

She whose body is 'hrīm'.

101. Om hakāra rūpāyai namaḥ

She who is of the letter 'ha'. (This letter indicates the valour which kills enemies. It is the sixth letter of the 'pañcadasākṣari' mantra.)

102. Om hala dhṛt pūjitāyai namaḥ

She who is worshipped by Balarāma (elder brother of Sri Krishna).

103. Om hariṇekṣaṇāyai namaḥ

She whose eyes are like a deer's.

104. Om hara priyāyai namaḥ

She who is the beloved of Shiva.

105. Om harārādhyāyai namaḥ
She who is worshipped by Shiva.

106. Om hari brahmendra vanditāyai namaḥ
She who is worshipped by Vishnu, Brahma and Indra.

107. Om hayā rūḍhā sevitāṅghryai namaḥ
She who is worshiped by the horse mounted cavalry.

108. Om hayamedha samarcitāyai namaḥ
She who is worshipped by the Aswamedha sacrifice.

109. Om haryakṣa vāhanāyai namaḥ
She who rides the lion (Durga).

110. Om hamsa vāhanāyai namaḥ
She who rides the swan (Saraswati).

111. Om hata dānavāyai namaḥ
She by whom the demons were killed.

112. Om hatyādi pāpa śamanyai namaḥ
She who destroys even grave sins such as killing.

113. Om harid aśvādi sevitāyai namaḥ
She who is worshipped by him who rides the green horse (Indra).

114. Om hasti kumbhottuṅga kucāyai namaḥ
She who has breasts as upright as the forehead of the elephant.

115. Om hasti kṛtti priyāṅganāyai namaḥ
She who is the darling of him who wears elephant skin (Shiva).

116. Om haridrā kumkumā digdhāyai namaḥ
She whose body is scented with turmeric powder and *kumkum* (saffron).

117. Om haryaśvādya marārcitāyai namaḥ
She who is worshipped by devas such as Indra.

118. Om harikeśa sakhyai namaḥ
She who is the friend of Shiva.

119. Om hādi vidyāyai namaḥ

She who is the science of the 'pañcadasākṣari' mantra.

120. Om hālā madollāsāyai namaḥ

She who is drunk with wine which was created from the ocean of milk.

121. Om sakāra rūpāyai namaḥ

She who is the letter 'sa'. (It denotes material wealth and pleasures and is the seventh letter of the 'pañcadasākṣari' mantra.)

122. Om sarvajñāyai namaḥ

She who is omniscient.

123. Om sarveśyai namaḥ

She who rules over all.

124. Om sarva maṅgalāyai namaḥ

She who is all auspiciousness.

125. Om sarva kartryai namaḥ

She who is the doer of all actions.

126. Om sarva bhartryai namaḥ
She who protects eveything.

127. Om sarva hantryai namaḥ
She who destroys everything.

128. Om sanātanāyai namaḥ
She who is eternal.

129. Om sarvānavadyāyai namaḥ
She who has no fault at all.

130. Om sarvāṅga sundaryai namaḥ
She whose entire form is beautiful.

131. Om sarva sākṣiṇyai namaḥ
She who is the witness of everything.

132. Om sarvātmikāyai namaḥ
She who is the essence of everything.

133. Om sarva saukhya dātryai namaḥ
She who gives all happiness.

134. Om sarva vimohinyai namaḥ
She who deludes all.

135. Om sarvādhārāyai namaḥ
She who is the substratum of everything.

136. Om sarva gatāyai namaḥ
She who is all pervading.

137. Om sarva viguṇa varjitāyai namaḥ
She who is devoid of defects.

138. Om sarvāruṇāyai namaḥ
She whose body is slightly reddish.

139. Om sarva mātre namaḥ
She who is the mother of all.

140. Om sarva bhūṣaṇa bhūṣitāyai namaḥ

She who is decorated with all ornaments.

141. Om kakārārthāyai namaḥ

She who is the meaning of the letter 'ka'. (This letter 'ka' represents light and is the eighth letter of the 'pañcadasākṣari' mantra.)

142. Om kāla hantryai namaḥ

She who is the destroyer of death.

143. Om kāmeṣyai namaḥ

She who controls all desires.

144. Om kāmitārthadāyai namaḥ

She who grants the objects of desire.

145. Om kāma sañjīvanyai namaḥ

She who brought the god of love back to life.

146. Om kalyāyai namaḥ

She who is capable of creation.

147. Om kaṭhina stana maṇḍalāyai namaḥ
She who has firm breasts.

148. Om kara bhorave namaḥ
She who has thighs like the elephant's trunk.

149. Om kalā nāthā mukhyai namaḥ
She whose face is like the full moon.

150. Om kaca jitāmbudāyai namaḥ
She who has hair which resembles the dark cloud.

151. Om kaṭākṣa syandi karuṇāyai namaḥ
She whose glance is full of compassion.

152. Om kapāli prāṇa nāyikāyai namaḥ
She who is the wife of Lord Shiva.

153. Om kāruṇya vigrahāyai namaḥ
She who is the personification of compassion.

154. Om kāntāyai namaḥ

She who is beautiful.

155. Om kānti bhūta japāvalyai namaḥ

She whose luster is like the hibiscus flower.

156. Om kalālāpāyai namaḥ

She who engages in the arts.

157. Om kambu kaṇṭhyai namaḥ

She whose neck has folds like a spiral shell.

158. Om kara nirjita pallavāyai namaḥ

She whose hands are softer than tender leaf buds.

159. Om kalpa vallī sama bhujāyai namaḥ

She whose arms are like wish-fulfilling creepers.

160. Om kastūri tilakāñcitāyai namaḥ

She who wears a dot of musk in between the eyebrows.

161. Om hakārārthāyai namaḥ

She who is the meaning of the letter 'ha'. (This letter 'ha' represents money, valour etc. and is the ninth letter of the 'pañcadasākṣari' mantra.

162. Om hamsa gatyai namaḥ

She who moves like a swan.

163. Om hāṭakābharaṇojjvalāyai namaḥ

She who shines wearing gold ornaments.

164. Om hāra hāri kucā bhogāyai namaḥ

She whose breasts are decorated by beautiful garlands.

165. Om hākinyai namaḥ

She who cuts the bondages.

166. Om halya varjitāyai namaḥ

She who is devoid of bad qualities.

167. Om haritpati samārādhyāyai namaḥ

She who is being worshipped by those eight gods who guard the different directions *(dig palakas)*.

168. Om haṭhātkāra hatāsurāyai namaḥ

She who killed *asuras* quickly by her valour.

169. Om harṣa pradāyai namaḥ

She who gives happiness.

170. Om havir bhoktryai namaḥ

She who partakes the offering given to sacrifice in fire.

171. Om hārda santamas āpahāyai namaḥ

She who removes darkness from the heart.

172. Om hallīsa lāsya santuṣṭāyai namaḥ

She who is pleased with *rasa lila*.

173. Om hamsa mantrārtha rūpiṇyai namaḥ

She who is the meaning of the '*hamsa*' mantra ('*So ham*', 'I am He').

174. Om hānopādāna vinirmuktāyai namaḥ

She who is free from loss and gain.

175. Om harṣiṇyai namaḥ

She who is delighted.

176. Om hari sodaryai namaḥ

She who is the sister of Lord Vishnu.

177. Om hāhā hūhū mukha stutyāyai namaḥ

She who is being praised by celestial beings called Hāhā and Hūhū.

178. Om hāni vṛddhi vivārjitāyai namaḥ

She who is beyond destruction and growth.

179. Om hayyaṅgavīna hṛdayāyai namaḥ

She who has a heart that melts like butter.

180. Om harigopāruṇāmśukāyai namaḥ

She who is of red colour.

181. Om lakārākhyāyai namaḥ

She whose is the letter ‘la’. (This is the tenth letter of the ‘pañcadasākṣari’ mantra.)

182. Om latā pūjyāyai namaḥ

She who is being worshipped by chaste women.

183. Om laya sthityut bhav eśvaryai namaḥ

She who is the controller of dissolution, sustainment and manifestation.

184. Om lāsya darśana santuṣṭāyai namaḥ

She who becomes pleased by seeing dance.

185. Om lābhālābha vivarjitāyai namaḥ

She who has neither gain nor loss.

186. Om laṅghyetarājñāyai namaḥ

She who does not obey others’ orders.

187. Om lāvaṇya śalinyai namaḥ

She who is of unmatched beauty.

188. Om laghu siddhidāyai namaḥ
She who gives attainments easily.

189. Om lākṣā rasa savarṇābhāyai namaḥ
She who shines like the color of *lākṣā*-juice (a bright violet plant).

190. Om lakṣmaṇāgraja pūjitāyai namaḥ
She who was worshipped by Lord Rama (elder brother of Lakshmana).

191. Om labhyetarāyai namaḥ
She who is attainable by others.

192. Om labdha bhakti sulabhāyai namaḥ
She who can be easily attained by devotion (*bhakti*).

193. Om lāṅgalāyudhāyai namaḥ
She who has a plough as a weapon (in her form of Adisesha).

194. Om lagna cāmara hasta śrī śāradā parivījitāyai namaḥ
She who is served by Lakshmi and Saraswati.

195. Om lajjāpada samārādhyāyai namaḥ

She who is worshipped by those who are modest.

196. Om lampaṭāyai namaḥ

She who has hidden herself from the earthly principles.

197. Om lakuleśvaryai namaḥ

She in whom the communities in the world merge.

198. Om labdha mānāyai namaḥ

She who is praised by all.

199. Om labdha rasāyai namaḥ

She who has attained the ultimate bliss.

200. Om labdha sampat samunnatyai namaḥ

She who has the apex of wealth.

201. Om hrīmkāriṇyai namaḥ

She who is the letter 'hrìm'. (This is the eleventh letter of the 'pañcadasākṣari' mantra.)

202. Om hrīmkārādyāyai namaḥ
She who is the origin of 'hrīm'.

203. Om hrīm madhyāyai namaḥ
She who is in the midst of 'hrīm'.

204. Om hrīm śikhāmaṇyai namaḥ
She who wears 'hrīm' in her head.

205. Om hrīmkāra kuṇḍāgni śikhāyai namaḥ
She who is the flame of the fire place (*homa kundam*) called 'hrīm'.

206. Om hrīmkāra śaśi candrikāyai namaḥ
She who is the nectar-like rays of the moon called 'hrīm'.

207. Om hrīmkāra bhāskara rucyai namaḥ
She who is the blissful rays of the sun called 'hrīm'.

208. Om hrīmkārāmboda cañcalāyai namaḥ
She who is the ray of lightning of the black clouds called 'hrīm'.

209. Om hrīmkāra kandāmkurikāyai namaḥ

She who is the germinating tendril of the tuber called 'hrīm'.

210. Om hrīmkāraika parāyaṇāyai namaḥ

She who completely relies on 'hrīm'.

211. Om hrīmkāra dīrghikā hamsyai namaḥ

She who is the swan playing in the canal called 'hrīm'.

212. Om hrīmkārodyāna kekinyai namaḥ

She who is the peahen playing in the garden of 'hrīm'.

213. Om hrīmkārāraṇya hariṇyai namaḥ

She who is the doe playing in the forest of 'hrīm'.

214. Om hrīmkārā lavā lavallyai namaḥ

She who is the ornamental climber in the flower bed of 'hrīm'.

215. Om hrīmkāra pañcara śukyai namaḥ

She who is the green parrot in the cage called 'hrīm'.

216. Om hrīmkārāṅgaṇa dīpikāyai namaḥ
She who is the light kept in the courtyard called 'hrīm'.

217. Om hrīmkāra kandarā simhyai namaḥ
She who is the lioness living in the cave called 'hrīm'.

218. Om hrīmkārāmbhoja bṛṅgikāyai namaḥ
She who is the insect playing in the lotus flower called 'hrīm'.

219. Om hrīmkāra sumano mādhvyai namaḥ
She who is the honey in the flower called 'hrīm'.

220. Om hrīmkāra taru mañjaryai namaḥ
She who is the flower bunch in the tree called 'hrīm'.

221. Om sakārākhyāyai namaḥ
She who is the letter 'sa'. (It is the twelfth letter of the 'pañcadasākṣari' mantra.)

222. Om samarasāyai namaḥ
She who is evenly blissful in all situations.

223. Om sakalāgama samstutāyai namaḥ
She who is praised by all Vedas.

224. Om sarva vedānta tātparya bhūmyai namaḥ
She who is the place which is the essence of all Vedanta.

225. Om sad asad āśrayāyai namaḥ
She who is the foundation of what is and what is not.

226. Om sakalāyai namaḥ
She who is everything.

227. Om saccidānandāyai namaḥ
She who is Existence, Consciousness and Bliss.

228. Om sādhyāyai namaḥ
She who is to be attained.

229. Om sad gati dāyinyai namaḥ
She who gives salvation.

230. Om sanakādi muni dhyeyāyai namaḥ
She who is meditated on by sages like Sanaka.

231. Om sadā śiva kuṭumbinyai namaḥ
She who is the wife of Shiva.

232. Om sakalādhiṣṭhāna rūpāyai namaḥ
She who is the substratum of everything.

233. Om satya rūpāyai namaḥ
She who is the personification of truth.

234. Om samā kṛtayai namaḥ
She whose form is evenly shaped.

235. Om sarva prapañca nirmātryai namaḥ
She who constructs the entire universe.

236. Om samānādhika varjitāyai namaḥ
She who has neither equal nor superior.

237. Om sarvottuṅgāyai namaḥ
She who is the greatest among all.

238. Om saṅga hīnāyai namaḥ
She who has no attachments to anything.

239. Om saguṇāyai namaḥ
She who has good qualities.

240. Om sakaleṣṭadāyai namaḥ
She who fulfills all desires.

241. Om kakāriṇyai namaḥ
She who is the letter 'ka'. (This is the thirteenth letter of the 'pañcadasākṣari' mantra.)

242. Om kāvya lolāyai namaḥ
She who enjoys poetry.

243. Om kāmeśvara manoharāyai namaḥ
She who steals the mind of Shiva.

244. Om kāmeśvara prāṇa nāḍyai namaḥ
She who is the life-nerve of Shiva.

245. Om kāmeśotsaṅga vāsinyai namaḥ
She who sits on the left lap of Shiva.

246. Om kāmeśvarāliṅgitāṅgyai namaḥ
She who is embraced by Shiva.

247. Om kāmeśvara sukha pradāyai namaḥ
She who gives happiness to Shiva.

248. Om kāmeśvara praṇayinyai namaḥ
She who is the beloved of Shiva.

249. Om kāmeśvara vilāsinyai namaḥ
She who is the divine play of Shiva.

250. Om kāmeśvara tapaḥ siddhyai namaḥ
She who achieved Shiva through austerities.

251. Om kāmeśvara manaḥ priyāyai namaḥ
She who pleases the mind of Shiva.

252. Om kāmeśvara prāṇa nāthāyai namaḥ
She who is the life-controller of Shiva.

253. Om kāmeśvara vimohinyai namaḥ
She who deludes Shiva.

254. Om kāmeśvara brahma vidyāyai namaḥ
She who is the Absolute knowledge of Shiva.

255. Om kāmeśvara gṛheśvaryai namaḥ
She who is the lord of the house of Shiva.

256. Om kāmeśvarāhlāda karyai namaḥ
She who makes Shiva supremely happy.

257. Om kāmeśvara maheśvaryai namaḥ
She who is Shiva's Goddess.

258. Om kāmeśvaryai namaḥ

She who is Kameshwari, consort of Shiva.

259. Om kāma koṭi nilayāyai namaḥ

She who presides over the kāma kōṭi pīṭa in Kāñchīpuram.

260. Om kāṅkṣitārthadāyai namaḥ

She who fulfills the desires of devotees.

261. Om lakāriṇyai namaḥ

She who is the letter 'la'. (This is the fourteenth letter of the 'pañcadasākṣari' mantra.)

262. Om labdha rūpāyai namaḥ

She who has assumed a form.

263. Om labdha dhiyai namaḥ

She who is full of wisdom.

264. Om labdha vāñchitāyai namaḥ

She whose desires are all fulfilled.

265. Om labdha pāpa mano dūrāyai namaḥ
She who is far away from the reach of sinners.

266. Om labdhāhaṅkāra durgamāyai namaḥ
She who is difficult to attain by the egoistic.

267. Om labdha śaktyai namaḥ
She who has all powers.

268. Om labdha dehāyai namaḥ
She who assumes a body.

269. Om labdhaīśvarya samunnatyai namaḥ
She who has all glories.

270. Om labdha vṛddhyai namaḥ
She who has all prosperity.

271. Om labdha līlāyai namaḥ
She who enacts a play.

272. Om labdha yauvana śālinyai namaḥ
She who is ever young.

273. Om labdhātiśaya sarvāṅga saundaryāyai namaḥ
She who possesses astounding beauty of form.

274. Om labdha vibhramāyai namaḥ
She who enacts the play of maintaining the world.

275. Om labdha rāgāyai namaḥ
She who exists as love.

276. Om labdha pataye namaḥ
She who has Shiva as her husband.

277. Om labdha nānāgama sthityai namaḥ
She who manifests all Vedas.

278. Om labdha bhogāyai namaḥ
She who experiences all.

279. Om labdha sukhāyai namaḥ

She who enjoys happiness.

280. Om labdha harṣābhi pūritāyai namaḥ

She who is overfilled with delight.

281. Om hrīmkāra mūrtyai namaḥ

She who is the personification of the sound 'hrīm'. (This is the fifteenth and last letter of the 'pañcadasākṣari' mantra.)

282. Om hrīmkāra saudha śṛiṅga kapotikāyai namaḥ

She who is the dove who lives in the top of the palace called 'hrīm'.

283. Om hrīmkāra dugdhābdhi sudhāyai namaḥ

She who is the nectar churned from the ocean of milk called 'hrīm'.

284. Om hrīmkāra kamalendirāyai namaḥ

She who is Goddess Lakshmi sitting on the lotus called 'hrīm'.

285. Om hrīmkāra maṇi dīparciṣe namaḥ

She who is the light of the ornamental lamp called 'hrīm'.

286. Om hrīmkāra taru śārikāyai namaḥ
She who is the lady bird sitting on the tree called 'hrīm'.

287. Om hrīmkāra peṭaka maṇyai namaḥ
She who is the pearl locked in the box called 'hrīm'.

288. Om hrīmkārādarśa bimbitāyai namaḥ
She who is the image reflected in the mirror called 'hrīm'.

289. Om hrīmkāra kośāsilatāyai namaḥ
She who is the shining sword in the sheath of 'hrīm'.

290. Om hrīmkārāsthāna nartakyai namaḥ
She who is the dancer on the stage called 'hrīm'.

291. Om hrīmkāra śuktikā muktāmaṇaye namaḥ
She who is the pearl found in the oyster shell called 'hrīm'.

292. Om hrīmkāra bodhitāyai namaḥ
She who is indicated by the sound 'hrīm'.

293. Om hrīmkāramaya sauvarṇa stambha vidruma putrikāyai namaḥ
She who is the coral statue on the shining pillars called ‘hrīm’.

294. Om hrīmkāra vedopaniṣade namaḥ
She who is the Upanishad in the Veda called ‘hrīm’.

295. Om hrīmkārā dhvara dakṣiṇāyai namaḥ
She who is the money gifted in the gate called ‘hrīm’.

296. Om hrīmkāra nandanārāma nava kalpaka vallaryai namaḥ
She who is the new divine climber present in the garden called ‘hrīm’.

297. Om hrīmkāra himavad gaṅgāyai namaḥ
She who is the river Ganga in the Himalaya mountain called ‘hrīm’.

298. Om hrīmkārārṇava kaustubhāyai namaḥ
She who is the precious gem given birth by the ocean called ‘hrīm’.

299. Om hrīmkāra mantra sarvasvāyai namaḥ
She who is the total wealth churned out of the mantra ‘hrīm’.

300. Om hrīmkārapara saukhyadāyai namaḥ

She who gives the infinite happiness of 'hrīm'.

Ārati

Hymn to Amma sung during *ārati* (the waving of burning camphor) followed by the Closing Prayers.

Om jaya jaya jagad jananī vande amṛtānandamayī
maṅgala ārati mātaḥ bhavāni amṛtānandamayī
mātā amṛtānandamayī /1

Victory to the Mother of the Universe. Obeisance to You Amritanandamayi. Most auspicious arati to You, Mother Bhavani.

jana mana nija śukhadāyini mātā amṛtānandamayī
maṅgala kāriṇi vande jananī amṛtānandamayī
mātā amṛtānandamayī /2

Adorations to the Giver of real happiness to the people, the Giver of all good things.

Sakalāgama niga mādiṣu carite amṛtānandamayī
nikhilāmaya hara jananī vande amṛtānandamayī
mātā amṛtānandamayī /3

You are the One glorified in the Vedas and Sastras. Adorations to You who destroys all unhappiness.

prema rasāmṛta varṣini mātā amṛtānandamayī
prema bhakti sandāyini mātā amṛtānandamayī
mātā amṛtānandamayī /4

You pour forth the nectar of Love, O Giver of unconditional Love.

śamadama dāyini manalaya kāriṇi amṛtānandamayī
satatam mama hṛdi vasatām devi amṛtānandamayī
mātā amṛtānandamayī /5

You are the Giver of inner and outer control. O You who dissolves the mind, O Devi, kindly reside always in my heart.

Patitoddhāra nirantara hṛdaye amṛtānandamayī
paramahamsa pada nilaye devī amṛtānandamayī
mātā amṛtānandamayī /6

In Your heart Your aim is to lift the fallen ones.
Established You are in the state of a paramahamsa.

he jananī jani maraṇa nivāriṇi amṛtānandamayī
he śrita jana paripālini jayatām amṛtānandamayī
mātā amṛtānandamayī /7

O Mother, who saves one from the cycle of birth and death,
who fosters all those who seek Your protection.

sura jana pūjita jaya jagadambā amṛtānandamayī
sahaja samādhi sudanye devī amṛtānandamayī
ātā amṛtānandamayī /8

You are the One worshipped by the gods, fulfilled and established in the natural state of samadhi.

om jaya jaya jagad jananī vande amṛtānandamayī
maṅgala ārati mātaḥ bhavāni amṛtānandamayī
mātā amṛtānandamayī /1

Victory to the Mother of the Universe. Obeisance to You Amritanandamayi. Most auspicious arati to You, Mother Bhavani.

Jai bolo sadguru mātā amṛtānandamayī devī kī

(Leader:) Say 'Victory to the Truth Teacher Mata Amritanandamayi Devi!'

Jai

Victory!

Bhagavad Gītā – Chapter 8

Chanted in Amritapuri on special occasions such as funeral rites

Athāṣṭo'dhyāyaḥ akṣarabrahma yogaḥ

Eighth chapter, 'The Yoga of the Imperishable Brahman'

Arjuna uvāca

Arjuna said:

Kim tad brahma kim adhyātmam/kim karma puruṣottama
adhibhūtam ca kim proktam/adhidaivam kim ucyate /1

What is that Brahman? What is the Adhyatma (the essential Self)? What is action? O best among men, what is declared to be the Abhibhoota (the Lord of beings)? And what is Adhidaiva (Lord of Gods) said to be?

Adhiyajñaḥ katham ko'tra/dehe'smin madhusūdana
prayāṇakāle ca katham/jñeyo'si niyatātmabhiḥ /2

When and how is Adhiyajna here in this body, O destroyer of Madhu? And how, at the time of death, are You to be known by the self controlled?

Śrī Bhagavān uvāca

The Blessed Lord said:

Akṣaram brahma paramam/svabhāvo'dhyātmam ucyate
bhūta bhāvod bhava karo/visargaḥ karma saṁjñitaḥ /3

Brahman is the Imperishable, the Supreme, His essential nature is called Self knowledge. The creative force that causes beings to spring forth into manifestation is called work.

Adhibhūtam kṣaro bhāvaḥ/puruṣaś cādhidaivatam
adhiyajño'ham evātra/dehe dehabhṛtām vara /4

Adhiboota constitutes My perishable nature and the Indweller is the Adhidaivata. I alone am the Adhiyajna here in this body, O Arjuna.

Antakāle ca māmeva/smaran muktvā kalevaram
yaḥ prayāti sa madbhāvam/yāti nāstyatra saṁśayaḥ /5

And whosoever leaving the body goes forth remembering Me alone, at the time of death he attains My being. There is no doubt about this.

Yam yam vāpi smaran bhāvam/tyajatyante kalevaram
tam tam evaiti kaunteya/sadā tadbhāvabhāvitaḥ /6

Whosoever, upon leaving the body, he goes to whatever being he dwells upon. This is because of his constant thought upon that being.

Tasmāt sarveṣu kāleṣu/mām anusmara yudhya ca
mayy arpita mano buddhir/mām evaiṣyasy asaṁśayaḥ /7

Therefore, at all times, remember Me and fight. With mind and intellect fixed on Me, you shall doubtless come to Me alone.

Abhyāsa yoga yuktena/cetasā nānya gāminā
paramam puruṣam divyam/yāti pārthānucintayan /8

One who withdraws the mind from all distractions, holds it steadfast through the method of habitual meditation and constantly meditates on the Supreme Purusha, the Resplendent, such a person goes to the Supreme.

Kavim purāṇam anuśāsitāram aṇor anīyāṁsam anusmared yaḥ sarvasya dhātāram acintya rūpam āditya varṇam tamasaḥ parastāt /9

Whosoever meditates upon the Omniscient, the Ancient, the Ruler, That which is more minute than an atom, the Supporter of all, of inconceivable form, effulgent like the sun and beyond darkness.

Prayāṇa kāle manasācalena bhaktyā yukto yoga balena caiva bhruvor madhye prāṇam āveśya saṁyak sa tam param puruṣam upaiti divyam /10

At the time of death, with an unshaken mind full of devotion, fixing the life energy between the eyebrows with the power of yoga, such a one reaches the resplendent, supreme Purusha

Yad akṣaram vedavido vadanti/ viśanti yad yatayo vītarāgāḥ yad icchanto brahmacaryam caranti/ tat te padam saṅgraheṇa pravakṣye /11

That which is declared Imperishable by those knowledgeable in the Veda, that which the self controlled and those free of desire enter, that desiring which Brahmacharya is practised, that goal I will declare to you in brief.

Sarva dvārāṇi saṁyamya/mano hṛdi nirudhya ca
mūrdhny ādhāyātmanaḥ prāṇam/āsthito yogadhāraṇām /12

Controlling all of the senses, having confined the mind in the heart, centering the life energy within, engaged in the practice of concentration.

Om ity ekākṣaram brahma/vyāharan mām anusmaran
yaḥ prayāti tyajan deham/sa yāti paramām gatim /13

Uttering the one syllabled 'Om', the symbol of Brahman, and remembering Me, such a one attains the Supreme goal when departing from the body.

Ananya cetāḥ satatam yo/mām smarati nityaśaḥ
tasyāham sulabhaḥ pārtha/nitya yuktasya yoginaḥ /14

I am easily attainable by that Yogi, ever steadfast, who constantly remembers Me, every day, without thinking of anything else, O Arjuna.

Mām upetya punar janma/duḥkhālayam aśāśvatam
nāpnuvanti mahātmānaḥ/saṁsiddhim paramām gatāḥ /15

Having attained Me, these great souls do not take birth again in this ephemeral abode of pain. They attain the highest perfection.

Ābrahma bhuvanāl lokāḥ/punar āvartino'rjuna
mām upetya tu kaunteya/punar janma na vidyate /16

All the worlds up to and including that of Brahma, the creator, are subject to rebirth, O Arjuna. But he who reaches Me is never reborn.

Sahasra yuga paryantam/ahar yad brahmaṇo viduḥ
rātrim yuga sahasrāntām/te'ho rātra vido janāḥ /17

Those who know the length of the Day of Brahma and the Night of Brahma, which each lasts for a thousand eons, they know day and night.

Avyaktād vyaktayaḥ sarvāḥ/prabhavanty aharāgame
rātry āgame pralīyante/tatraivāvyakta sāṁjñake /18

From the unmanifested all the manifested proceed at the coming of the Day. At the coming of Night they dissolve into that same unmanifested.

Bhūta grāmaḥ sa evāyam/bhūtvā bhūtvā pralīyate
rātry āgame'vaśaḥ pārtha/prabhavaty ahar āgame /19

The multitude of beings are helplessly bom and dissolved again and again, O Arjuna, during the successive days and nights of Brahma.

Paras tasmāt tu bhāvo'nyo/'vyakto'vyaktāt sanātanaḥ
yaḥ sa sarveṣu bhūteṣu/naśyatsu na vinaśyati /20

But verily there is the eternal existence beyond the unmanifest. It is not destroyed when all beings are destroyed.

Avyakto'kṣara ity uktas/tam āhuḥ paramām gatim
yam prāpya na nivartante/tad dhāma paramam mama /21

This Imperishable is the highest goal. They who reach it never return. That is My highest abode.

Puruṣaḥ sa paraḥ pārtha/bhaktyā labhyas tvananyayā
yasyāntaḥ sthāni bhūtāni/yena sarvam idam tatam /22

That highest Purusha, O Arjuna, is attainable through unswerving devotion to It. In That all beings dwell, by That all this is pervaded.

Yatra kāle tvanāvṛttim/āvṛttim caiva yoginaḥ
prayātā yānti tam kālam/vakṣyāmi bharatarṣabha /23

Now I will tell you at what time Yogins depart only to return again, and at what time Yogins depart never to return again.

Agnir jyotir ahaḥ śuklaḥ/ṣaṇmāsā uttarāyaṇam
tatra prayātā gacchanti/brahma brahma vido janāḥ /24

Fire, light, day-time, the bright fortnight and the six months of the northern solstice, following this path those who know Brahman go to Brahman.

Dhūmo rātris tathā kṛṣṇaḥ/ṣaṇmāsā dakṣiṇāyanam
tatra cāndramasam jyotir/yogī prāpya nivartate /25

Smoke, night time, the dark fortnight and the six months of the summer solstice, following this path and attaining the lunar light, the Yogin returns.

Śuklakṛṣṇe gatī hyete/jagataḥ śāśvate mate
ekayā yāty anāvṛttim/anyayā'vartate punaḥ /26

The path of light and the path of darkness, both available to the world, are eternal. By the path of light, a man goes and does not return; from the path of darkness he returns again.

Naite sṛtī pārtha jānan/yogī muhyati kaścana
tasmāt sarveṣu kāleṣu/yogayukto bhavārjuna /27

Knowing these paths, O Arjuna, no Yogin is deluded. Therefore, at all times be steadfast in Yoga.

Vadeṣu yajñeṣu tapaḥsu caiva dāneṣu yat puṇya phalam pradiṣṭam
atyeti tat sarvam idam viditvā yogī param sthānam upaiti cādyam /28

Whatever merit one attains through study of the Vedas, from the performance of sacrifices or from the practice of austerities and charity, beyond the attainment of this merit goes the Yogin who, having known these two paths, attains to the Supreme.

Om tat sat iti śrīmad bhagavadgītāsu
upaniṣadsu brahma vidyāyām
yoga śāstre śrī kṛṣṇārjuna saṁvāde
akṣarabrahma yogo nāmāṣṭo'dhyāyaḥ

Thus, in the Upanishad sung by the Lord, the science of Brahman, the scripture of Yoga, the dialogue between Sri Krishna and Arjuna, ends the eighth chapter, entitled 'The Yoga of the Imperishable Brahman'

Om sarva dharmān parityajya mām ekam śaraṇam vraja
aham tvā sarva pāpebhyo mokṣayiṣyāmi mā śucaḥ (Ch. 18.66)

Relinquishing all dharmas take refuge in Me alone. I will liberate you from all sins; do not grieve.

Bhagavad Gītā – Chapter 15

Chanted in Amritapuri before meals, followed by Yagna Mantra

Atha pañcadaśo'dhyāyaḥ puruśottama yogaḥ

Fifteenth chapter, 'The Yoga of the Supreme Person'

Śrī bhagavān uvāca

The Blessed Lord said

Ūrdhva mūlam adhaḥ-śākham/aśvattham prāhur avyayam
chandāṁsi yasya parṇāni/yas tam veda sa veda vit /1

He who knows the Peepul tree, which is said to be imperishable, whose roots are in the Primeval Being, whose stem is represented by Brahma, whose leaves are the Vedas, is a knower of the Vedas.

Adhaś cordhvam prasṛtās tasya śākhā guṇa-pravṛddhā viṣaya-pravālāḥ
adhaś ca mālāny-anusantatānikarmānubandhīni manuṣya-loke /2

Fed by the three gunas and having the sense objects for leaves, the branches of the aforesaid tree extend both downwards and upwards. Its roots, which bind the soul according to its actions in the human body, are spread in all regions, higher as well as lower.

Na rūpam asyeha tathopalabhyate nānto na cādir na ca sampratiṣṭhā
aśvattham enam suvirūḍha mūlam asaṅga śastreṇa dṛḍhena chittvā /3

The nature of this tree of creation does not, upon mature thought, turn out to be what it seems to represent. It has neither beginning nor end nor even stability. Therefore, felling this firmly rooted Peepul tree with the ax of dispassion, ...

Tataḥ padam tat parimārgitavyam yasmin gatā na nivartanti bhūyaḥ
tam eva cādyam puruṣam prapadye yataḥ pravṛttiḥ prasṛtā purāṇī /4

... diligently seek for that supreme state. One who attains to that state returns no more to this world. Having fully dedicated oneself to that Primeval Being, from whom the flow of this beginningless creation has progressed, one should dwell on and meditate on Him.

Nirmāna-mohā jita-saṅga-doṣā adhyātma-nityā vinivṛtta-kāmāḥ
dvandvair vimuktāḥ sukha-duḥkha-saṁjñair gaccanty-amūḍhāḥ
padam avyayam tat /5

Those wise men who are free from pride and delusion, who have conquered the evil of attachment, who are in eternal union with God, whose cravings have ceased and who are immune to the pairs of opposites of pleasure and pain, reach that supreme immortal state.

Na tad bhāsayate sūryo/na śaśāṅko na pāvakaḥ
yad gatvā na nivartante/tad dhāma paramam mama /6

Neither the sun nor the moon nor even fire can illumine that supreme, self effulgent state. Attaining to that, one never returns to this world. That is My supreme abode.

Mamaivāṁśo jīva-loke/jīva bhūtaḥ sanātanaḥ
manaḥ-ṣaṣṭhānīndriyāṇi/prakṛti-sthāni karṣati /7

The eternal life force in each body is a particle of My own being. It is that alone which draws round itself the mind and the five senses which rest in nature.

Śarīram yad avāpnoti/yac cāpy-utkrāmatīśvaraḥ
gṛhītvaitāni saṁyāti/vāyur gandhān ivāśayāt /8

As the wind lifts scents from their place of origin, so the life force in and controller of the body takes the mind and senses with it when it leaves one body and migrates to another.

Śrotram cakṣuḥ sparśanam ca/rasanam ghrāṇam eva ca
adhiṣṭhāya manaś cāyam/viṣayān upasevate /9

It is while dwelling in the senses of hearing, touch, taste, sight and smell, as well as in the mind that the life force enjoys the objects of the senses.

Utkrāmantam sthitam vāpi/bhuñjānam vā guṇānvitam
vimūḍhā nānupaśyanti/paśyanti jñāna-cakṣuṣaḥ /10

The ignorant know not the soul that departs from and dwells in the body and enjoys the objects of the senses. Only those endowed with the eye of wisdom are able to see it.

Yatanto yoginaś cainam/paśyanty-ātmany-avasthitam
yatanto'py-akṛtātmāno/nainam paśyanty-acetasaḥ /11

Striving Yogis see the Self enshrined in their heart. The ignorant one, whose heart has not been purified, knows not the Self in spite of their best efforts.

Yad āditya-gatam tejo/jagad bhāsayate'khilam
yac candramasi yac cāgnau/tat tejo viddhi māmakam /12

The light in the sun that illumines the whole world, the light in the moon and the light in the fire, know that light to be Mine alone.

Gām āviśya ca bhūtāni/dhārayāmy-aham ojasā
puṣṇāmi cauṣadhīḥ sarvāḥ/somo bhūtvā rasātmakaḥ /13

Permeating the soil, it is I who support all creatures by My vital power. Becoming the nectarous moon, I nourish all of the plants.

Aham vaiśvānaro bhūtvā/prāṇinām deham āśritaḥ
prāṇāpāna-samāyuktaḥ/pacāmy-annam catur-vidham /14

Taking the form of fire lodged in the body of all creatures and united with their exhalations and inhalations, it is I who consume the four kinds of food.

Sarvasya cāham hṛdi sanniviṣṭo mattaḥ smṛtir jñānam apohanam ca
vedaiś ca sarvair aham eva vedyo vedānta kṛd veda vid eva cāham /15

It is I who remain seated in the heart of all creatures; I am the inner controller of all. I am the source of memory, knowledge and reason. I am the only object worth knowing through the Vedas. I am the father of the Vedas and the knower of the Vedas also.

Dvāv imau puruṣau loke/kṣaraś cākṣara eva ca
kṣaraḥ sarvāṇi bhūtāni/kūṭa-stho'kṣara ucyate /16

There are two beings in this world, the Perishable and the Imperishable. The bodies of all beings are the Perishable; the embodied soul is the Imperishable.

Uttamaḥ puruṣas tvanyaḥ/paramātmety-udāhṛtaḥ
yo loka-trayam āviśya/bibharty-avyaya īśvaraḥ /17

The Supreme Person is yet other than these. He, having entered all the three worlds, upholds and maintains all. He is spoken of as the Imperishable Lord and the Supreme Spirit.

Yasmāt kṣaram atītoham/akṣarād api cottamaḥ
ato'smi loke vede ca/prathitaḥ puruṣottamaḥ /18

I am beyond both the Perishable and the Imperishable, thus I am known as the Supreme Person both in this world and in the Vedas.

Yo mām evam asammūḍho/jānāti puruṣottamam
sa sarva vid bhajati mām/sarva bhāvena bhārata /19

Arjuna, the wise person who thus realizes Me as the Supreme Person, he knows all and he constantly worships Me with his whole being.

Iti guhyatamam śāstram/idam uktam mayānaghatad buddhvā
buddhimān syāt/kṛta kṛtyaś ca bhārata /20

This most esoteric teaching has thus been imparted by Me. Grasping it in essence, a man becomes wise and his mission in life is accomplished.

Om tat sat, iti śrīmad bhagavadgītāsu upaniṣadsu brahma vidyāyām yoga śāstre śrī kṛṣṇārjuna saṁvāde puruṣottama yogo nāma pañcadaśo'dhyāyaḥ

Thus, in the Upanishad sung by the Lord, the science of Brahman, the scripture of Yoga, the dialogue between Sri Krishna and Arjuna, ends the fifteenth chapter, entitled 'The Yoga of the Supreme Person.'

Om sarva-dharmān parityajya mām ekam śaraṇam vraja
aham tvā sarva-pāpebhyo mokṣayiṣyāmi mā śucaḥ (Ch. 18.66)

Relinquishing all dharmas take refuge in Me alone. I will liberate you from all sins; do not grieve.

Yagna Mantra

Mantra of sacrifice, Bhagavad Gītā 4.24

Chanted in Amritapuri before meals

Om – Brahmārpaṇam brahma havir brahmāgnau brahmaṇā hutam
brahmaiva tena gantavyam brahma karma samādhinā
Om śāntiḥ śāntiḥ śāntiḥ
Om śrī gurubhyo namaḥ - harī om

Om, Brahman is the giving, Brahman is the food offering,
by Brahman it is offered into the Brahman fire,
Brahman is that which is to be attained by complete absorption in Brahman action.
Om peace, peace, peace
Om, reverence to the auspicious gurus. Hari Om

Guru Stotram

Akhaṇḍamaṇḍalākaram/vyāptam yena carācaram
tatpadam darśitam yena/tasmai śrī gurave namaḥ /1

Salutations to the Guru who reveals the supreme, undivided essence that pervades this entire universe of moving and non-moving beings.

Ajñāna timirāndhasya/jñānāñjana śalākayā
cakṣurunmīlitam yena/tasmai śrī gurave namaḥ /2

Salutations to the Guru who rescues us from the darkness of ignorance and restores to us the vision of knowledge and of the Truth.

Gururbrahmā gururviṣṇuḥ/gururdevo maheśvaraḥ
guru sākṣāt param brahma/tasmai śrī gurave namaḥ /3

Salutations to the Guru who is Brahma, Visnu and Shiva. The Guru is the Supreme Brahman itself.

Sthāvaram jaṅgamam vyāptam/yatkiñcit sacarācaram
tatpadam darśitam yena/tasmai śrī gurave namaḥ /4

Salutations to the Guru who reveals the essence of all beings, whether they be in motion or still, alive or dead.

Cinmayam vyāpiyat sarvam/trailokyam sacarācaram
tatpadam darśitam yena/tasmai śrī gurave namaḥ /5

Salutations to the Guru who reveals the pure intelligence that animates all of the moving and the non-moving beings in the three worlds.

Sarva śruti śiroratna/virājita padāmbujaḥ
vedāntāmbuja sūryo yaḥ/tasmai śrī gurave namaḥ /6

Salutations to the Guru whose blessed feet are adorned with the gems that are the revelations of the scriptures. The Guru is the sun that causes the flower of knowledge to bloom.

Caitanya śāśvata śānta/vyomātīto nirañjanaḥ
bindunādakalātītaḥ/tasmai śrī gurave namaḥ /7

Salutations to the Guru who is intelligence itself, who is the eternal, who dwells in everlasting peace and bliss beyond space and time, who is pure and who is beyond all sounds and vision.

Jñānaśakti samārūḍhaḥ/tattvamālā vibhūṣitaḥ
bhukti mukti pradātā ca/tasmai śrī gurave namaḥ /8

Salutations to the Guru who wields the power of knowledge, who is adorned with a garland of the gems of truth and who grants both material prosperity and spiritual liberation.

Anekajanma samprāpta/karmabandha vidāhine
ātma jñānā pradānena/tasmai śrī gurave namaḥ /9

Salutations to the Guru who reveals the light of knowledge and thus destroys the evil fate that has accumulated during countless births.

Śoṣaṇam bhavasindhośca/jñāpanam sārasampadaḥ
guroḥ pādodakam samyak/tasmai śrī gurave namaḥ /10

Salutations to the Guru, the water sanctified by the touch of whose feet dries up the ocean of illusion and reveals the true and only contentment.

Na guroradhikam tattvam/na guroradhikam tapaḥ
tattvajñānāt param nāsti/tasmai śrī gurave namaḥ /11

There is no truth as high as that of the Guru, there is no tapas higher than the Guru, there is no higher knowledge than His. Salutations to the Guru.

Mannāthaḥ śrī jagannāthaḥ/madguruḥ śrī jagadguruḥ
madātmā sarvabhūtātmā/tasmai śrī gurave namaḥ /12

My Lord is the Lord of the universe, my Guru is the Guru of the three worlds, my Self is the Self within all beings. Salutations to the Guru.

Gurur ādiranādiśca guruḥ/paramadaivatam
guroḥ parataram nāsti/tasmai śrī gurave namaḥ /13

Though He lives, He was never born; the Satguru is the supreme truth. Above all else in the universe is the Satguru. Salutations to the Guru.

Devī Bhujaṅgam

Ṣaḍādhāra paṅkeruhāntar virājat
suṣumnāntarāleti tejollasantīm
vibantīm sudhāmaṇḍalam drāvayantīm
sudha mūrti mīḍhe mahānanta rūpām /1

I bow before that personification of nectar, who is the ever lasting immortal bliss, who is the luster in the Sushumna, which is in the six chakras of the body, and who melts the moon and drinks its light.

Jvalat koṭi bālārka bhāsāruṇāṅgīm
sulāvaṇyaśṛṅgāra śobhābhirāmām
mahāpatma kiñjalkamadhye virājat
trikoṇollasantīm bhaje śrī bhavānīm /2

I sing about that Bhavani, who sits in the triangle, which shines in the stamen of the great lotus, who has the luster of crores of rising suns, who is immensely pretty, and who attracts the entire world by her charm.

Kvaṇal kiṅkiṇī nūvuro bhāsiranta
prabhālīḍha lākṣārdra pādāravindam
ajeśācyutādyais surais sevyamānām
mahādevi! manmūrdhni te bhāvayāmi /3

O great goddess, please keep Your feet, which have jingling bells made of gems tied to it, which shine in the luster of Your wet lac painted feet, and which are worshipped by Vishnu, Brahma and others, on my head and bless me.

Suśoṇāmbarā badhnī virājan
mahāratnakāñcīkalāpam nitambam
sphuraddakṣiṇāvartanābhiścatisro
valīramba! te romarājīm bhajeham /4

I worship the streak of hair on Your belly, Your shining navel circling to the left, Your hips dressed in red garments, and Your waist adorned with golden tinkling belt, studded with greatest of jewels.

Lasat vṛtta muttuṅga māṇikya kumbho
pama śrī stanadvantvam ambāmbujākṣi
bhaje dugdha pūrṇābhirāmam tvadīyam
mahā hāra dīptam sadā vismitāsyam /5

I worship Your twin radiant raised breasts full of milk, which are round and like the gem studded pot, and which are ever shining with milk. Hey Mother who has lotus-like eyes.

Śirīṣa prasūnollasal bāhū daṇḍair
jjvalalbāṇakodaṇḍa pāśāmkuśāśca
calalkaṅkaṇoddāma keyūra bhūṣol
lasac chrīkarām bhojamābāhumīḍe /6

I worship that Bhavani, who glitters with her arms, which are as delicate as Sirisha flowers, and which carry arrow, bow, noose and goad, and which shine with bangles and bracelets.

Sunāsāpuṭam patma patrā yatākṣam
mukham devi bhakteṣ ṭada śrī kaṭākṣam
lalāṭ ojjvalat gandha kastūribhūṣ
ojjvalat pūrṇa candra prabham te bhajeham /7

I worship that Bhavani, who is extremely pleasant, who shines like the full moon of autumn, whose lotus like face is adorned with peace, and who shines with a gem studded necklace and ear studs.

Calal kuntalānubhramal bhṛṅgavṛndair
ghanastigdha dhammila bhūṣojjvalantīm
sphuran mauli māṇikya baddhendurekhā
vilāsollasad divya murdhānamīḍe /8

I praise Your head, which is playfully radiant, which is adorned by the crescent moon, which is decorated by the line of gems, in whose dense hair the swarm of bees, enter, swirl and play, and which is decorated, by densely woven white jasmine flowers.

Iti śrī bhavānī svarūpam tavaivam
prapañcāl parañ cāti sūkṣmam prasannam
sphuratvamba! ḍimbhasya me hṛt saroje
sadā vāṅmayam sarva tejo maya tvam /9

This form of Yours, o Bhavani, which is much above the universe, in its micro form, may please shine in my lotus heart, and bless me in Your lustrous form, so that I rule over the wealth of words.

Gaṇeśāṇi mādyākhilaiś śakti vṛndaiḥ
Sphurat śrī mahā cakra rāje lasantīm
parām rājarājeśvarī traipurīm tvām
śivāṅkoparistham śivām tvam bhajeham /10

I meditate on You, the wife of Shiva, who is sitting pleasantly on his lap, surrounded by Shaktis led by Lord Ganesha, who is sitting highly radiant on the chakra raja, and who is Tripura and Rajarajeshvari.

Tvam arkas tvam agnis tvam āpas tvam indus
tvam ākāśa bhūr vāyu sarvam tvameva
tvadanyam na kiṅcil prakāśosti sarvam
sadānanda saṁvitsvarūpam bhajeham /11

I sing about You in a form of blissful knowledge, as to whom there is none superior. You are sun, fire, water, and moon, You are ether, earth, and wind, You are everything indeed, You are the great essence.

Śivas tvam gurus tvaṇca śaktis tvameva
tvamevāsi mātā pita ca tvameva
tvamevāsi vidyā tvamevāsi bandhur
gatiramme matirdevi sarvam tvameva /12

You are lord Shiva, You are my teacher, You are the Goddess Shakti. You are my mother, You are my father, You are the knowledge, You are my relations, and so You are my only refuge, my only thought. Everything that I can think of is You.

Śrutī nāmagamyam purāṇairagamyam
mahimnānu jānanti pāram tavātra
stutim kartumicchāmi te tvam bhavāni
kṣamasvaivam amba pramugdhaḥ kilāham /13

Though I don't know Your greatness, wish I to praise You, o Bhavani. You are the knower of Vedas and Agamas, and You are unreachable through scriptures. So please pardon me for doing this.

Śaraṇyai vareṇyai sukāruṇya pūrṇair
hiraṇyodarādyai ragaṇyais supūrṇaiḥ
bhavāraṇya bhītaśca mām pāhi bhadre
namaste namaste punaste namostu! /14

Salutations, salutations, and salutations, o Bhavani. You are my refuge, my boon and form of all mercy, You are greatest among all devas, o holy one, and so, please protect me from this forest snare of life.

Bhavānī bhavānī bhavānīti vaṇī
mudārāmudāram mudā ye bhajanti
na śoko na pāpo na rogo na mṛtyuḥ
kadācil kadacil kadacinnarāṇām /15

Three times repeat the holy name of Bhavani, with devotion and repeatedly for ever, and get rid of sorrow, passion, sin and fear, for all time and for all ways.

Idam śuddhacitto bhavānī bhujaṅgam
paṭhan buddhimān bhaktiyuktaśca tasmai
svakīyam padam śāśvatam vedasāram
śriyaṅceṣṭasiddhiśca devīdadāti /16

Who ever correctly reads with devotion, this great hymn praising Bhavani from head to toe, would attain a permanent place of salvation, which is the essence of Vedas, and also get wealth and the eight occult powers.

Annapūrṇa Stotram

Hymn to the All-Nourishing Mother

Nityānandakarī varābhayakarī saundaryaratnākarī
nirdhūtākhila ghora pāpanikarī pratyakṣa māheśvarī
prāleyācala vamśa pāvanakarī kāśīpuraādhīśvarī
bhikṣām dehi kṛpāvalambanakarī mātānnapūrṇeśvarī /1

O Mother Annapūrneshvari, please bestow alms upon me. You dispense eternal happiness as well as boons and protection. Our fears are dispelled by You. By washing away our sins You grant us mental purity. O great goddess, You purified the race of Himavan. Ruler of Kashi, You are the embodiment of mercy.

Nānāratna vicitrabhūṣaṇakarī hemāmbarāḍambarī
mūktāhāra vilambamāna vilasadvakṣojakumbhāntarī
kāṣmīrā garuvāsitā rucikarī kāśīpurādhīśvarī
bhikṣām dehi kṛpāvalambanakarī mātānnapūrṇeśvarī /2

O Mother Annapūrneshvari, please bestow alms upon me. Your hands are adorned with ornaments and jewels and You are beautifully clothed in golden attire. Upon Your breasts and waist rest garlands made of pearl. You are wonderfully fragrant with the frankincense of Kashmir, O incarnation of beauty. Ruler of Kashi, You are the embodiment of mercy.

Yogānandakarī ripukṣayakarī dharmaikaniṣṭhākarī
candrārkānalabhāsamānalaharī trailokyarakṣākarī
sarvaiśvarya karī tapaḥ phalakarī kāśīpurādhīśvarī
bhikṣām dehi kṛpāvalambanakarī mātānnapūrṇeśvarī /3

O Mother Annapūrneshvari, please bestow alms upon me. You dispense the bliss of Yoga. By Your grace our enemies are destroyed and our feet are set firmly on the path of dharma. You display the radiance of the moon, the sun and fire. The three worlds are protected by You. All prosperity and all of the rewards for penance flow from You. Ruler of Kashi, You are the embodiment of mercy.

Kailāsācala kandarālayakarī gaurī umā śaṅkarī
kaumārī nigamārthagocarakarī omkārabījākṣarī

mokṣadvārakavāṭapāṭanakarī kāśīpurādhīśvarī
bhikṣām dehi kṛpāvalambanakarī mātānnapūrṇeśvarī /4

O Mother Annapūrneshvari, please bestow alms upon me. You dwell amidst the caves of Mount Kailash. O Uma, You radiate a golden hue. Consort of Lord Shiva, blessed with eternal youth, You reveal the inner meaning of the Vedas. Embodiment of 'OM,' You open the door to eternal liberation. Ruler of Kashi, You are the embodiment of mercy.

Dṛśyādṛśya vibhūtivāhanakarī brahmāṇḍabhāṇḍodarī
līlānāṭaka sūtra bhedanakarī vijñānadīpāṅkurī
śrī viśveśāmanaḥ prasādakarī kāśīpurādhīśvarī
bhikṣām dehi kṛpāvalambanakarī mātānnapūrṇeśvarī /5

O Mother Annapūrneshvari, please bestow alms upon me. You grant all visible and invisible blessings. The entire universe is contained in You. This world is a drama that You have staged. You are the fire in the torch of wisdom. The mind of the Lord of the universe is pleased by You. Ruler of Kashi, You are the embodiment of mercy.

Urvīsarvajaneśvarī jayakarī mātākṛpāsāgarī
veṇīnīlasamānakuntaladharī nityānnadāneśvarī
sākṣānmokṣakarī sadā śubhakarī kāśīpurādhīśvarī
bhikṣām dehi kṛpāvalambanakarī mātānnapūrṇeśvarī /6

O Mother Annapūrneshvari, please bestow alms upon me. You are the queen of the world. Showering Your motherly love on all, You insure success. O ocean of kindness, with locks of beautiful hair arranged in braids, You provide the means of sustenance to all beings. Granting salvation to all, Your every action is auspicious. Ruler of Kashi, You are the embodiment of mercy.

Ādikṣānta samasta varṇanakari śambhostri bhāvākarī
kāśmīrā tripureśvarī triṇayanī viśveśvarī śarvarī
kāmākāṅkṣakarī janodayakarī kāśīpurādhīśvarī
bhikṣām dehi kṛpāvalambanakarī mātānnapūrṇeśvarī /7

O Mother Annapūrneshvari, please bestow alms upon me. The letters of the alphabet were first invented by You. You monitor Shambu's three-fold aspect of creation, protection and destruction. Covered in saffron, partner of the three-eyed destroyer of

Tripura, ruler of the universe, You perfect in Yourself the beauty of the night and You open wide the doors to heaven. Ruler of Kashi, You are the embodiment of mercy.

Devī sarva vicitraratnaracitā dākṣāyaṇī sundarī
vāmā svādupayodharā priyakarī saubhāgya māheśvarī
bhaktābhīṣṭakarī sadā śubhakarī kāśīpurādhīśvarī
bhikṣām dehi kṛpāvalambanakarī mātānnapūrṇeśvarī /8

O Mother Annapūrneshvari, please bestow alms upon me. O radiant one, adorned with a display of rare jewels, charming daughter of Daksha, You are blessed with perfect manners and noble virtues. Always engaged in auspicious acts, You grant the desires of those who earnestly open their hearts to You. Ruler of Kashi, You are the embodiment of mercy.

Candrārkānalakoṭi koṭisadṛśī candrām śubimbādharī
candrārkāgni samāna kuṇḍaladharī candrārkavarṇeśvarī
mālāpustakapāśasāṅkuśadharī kāśīpurādhīśvarī
bhikṣām dehi kṛpāvalambanakarī mātānnapūrṇeśvarī /9

O Mother Annapūrneshvari, please bestow alms upon me. The splendor of Your form is greater even than that of thousands of moons, suns and fires combined together. Your lips resemble rare and luscious fruit and are as pleasant as moonlight. In beauty You surpass the celestial orbs. In Your hands You clasp a garland, a book, a rope and a goad. Ruler of Kashi, You are the embodiment of mercy.

Kṣatratrāṇakarī mahābhayakarī mātā kṛpāsāgarī
sarvānandakarī sadā śivakarī viśveśvarīśrīdharī
dakṣākrandakarī nirāmayakarī kāśīpurādhīśvarī
bhikṣām dehi kṛpāvalambanakarī mātānnapūrṇeśvarī /10

O Mother Annapūrneshvari, please bestow alms upon me. You grant protection like a warrior and thus dispel all fears. O mother, ocean of kindness, You provide all with happiness. Auspicious one, You hold sway over this universe and control destiny. You brought great distress to Daksha Prajapati. All ailments are cured by You. Ruler of Kashi, You are the embodiment of mercy.

Annapūrṇe sadāpūrṇe śaṅkaraprāṇavallabhe
jñānavairāgya siddhyartham bhikṣām dehi ca pārvati /11

O Annapoorna, You are ever full. Radiating the essence of life, never exhausted, O partner of Shankara, grant to me that I become fully established in knowledge and renunciation.

Mātā me pārvatī devi pitā devo maheśvaraḥ
bāndhavāḥ śivabhaktāśca svadeśo bhuvanatrayam /12

Parvati Devi is my Divine Mother and Lord Mahesvara is my Father. My family encompasses the devotees of Shiva; all the three worlds are my native lands.

Closing Prayers

Om asatomā sadgamaya
tamasomā jyotirgamaya
mṛityormā amṛtamgamaya
om śāntiḥ śāntiḥ śāntiḥ

Om, lead us from untruth to Truth,
from darkness to light,
from death to immortality.
Om peace, peace, peace

Om lokāḥ samastāḥ sukhino bhavantū
lokāḥ samastāḥ sukhino bhavantū
lokāḥ samastāḥ sukhino bhavantū
om śāntiḥ śāntiḥ śāntiḥ

Om, may all the beings in all the worlds be happy!
Om peace, peace, peace

Om pūrṇamadaḥ pūrṇamidam
pūrṇāt pūrṇamudacyate
pūrṇasya pūrṇamādāya
pūrṇam-evā-vaśiśyate
om śāntiḥ śāntiḥ śāntiḥ

Om, That is the whole, this is the whole,
from the whole the whole becomes manifest
taking away the whole from the whole,
the whole remains.
Om peace, peace, peace

Om śrī gurubhyo namaḥ
harī om

Om, reverence to the auspicious gurus
Hari Om

Pronunciation Guide

Vowels can be short or long, o and e are always long in Sanskrit.

a - as u in but
ā - as a in far, long
i - as i in pin
ī - as ee in meet, long
u - as u in push
ū - as oo in hoot, long
ṛ - as ri in rim
e - as e in America, long
ai - as ai in aisle
o - as o in goal, long
au - as ow in cow
ṁ - before a guttural sound like ṅ, before a palate sound like ṇ, before a dental sound like n and before a lip sound like m.
ḥ - pronounce aḥ like aha, āḥ like āha, iḥ like ihi, uḥ. like uhu.
ḥ - is mute inside lines

Most consonants can be aspirated (*kh*) or not aspirated (*k*). The aspiration is part of the consonant, the examples given below are therefore only approximate.

k - as k in kite
kh - as ckh in Eckhart
g - as g in give
gh - as g-h in dig-hard
ṅ - as n in sing

c - as c in cello
ch - as ch-h in staunch-heart
j - as j in joy
jh - as dgeh in hedgehog
ñ - as ny in canyon

The letters d, t, n with dots under them are pronounced with the tip of the tongue against the roof of the mouth, the others with the tip against the teeth.

ṭ, t - as t in tub
ṭh, th - as th in lighthouse
ḍ, d - as d in dove
ḍh, dh - as dh in red-hot
ṇ, n - an n in naught

p - as p in pine
ph - as ph in up-hill
b - as b in bird
bh - as bh in rub-hard
m - as m in mother

y - as y in yes
r - as r in Italian Roma (rolled)
l - as l in like
v - as w in when
ṣ - as sh in shine
ś - as s in German sprechen
s - as s in sun
h - as h in hot

With double consonants the initial sound only is pronounced twice:

cc - as tc in hot chip
jj - as dj in red jet

Proper pronunciation surely requires some practice. Amma assures us however that the Divine Mother will still understand us if our pronunciation is faulty.

www.ingramcontent.com/pod-product-compliance
Lightning Source LLC
Chambersburg PA
CBHW070137100426
42743CB00013B/2732
9781680370072